What People Are Saying About

"What a beautiful book! Written without the trappings of spiritual or psychological jargon, *The Soulmate Experience* is a user-friendly guide to a completely authentic way of being. In a simple and personal way, Mali and Joe usher you into a new paradigm of relating where the truth of unconditional love can actually be known and lived."
~TOBIN GIBLIN, AUTHOR OF *THE ART OF MINDFUL LIVING*

"Mali and Joe get to the heart of the heart."
~FRANK FERRANTE, STAR OF *MAY I BE FRANK*

"Reading this book is like listening to your best friend who knows you better than anyone else and loves you unconditionally." ~LAURA ALAVOSUS

"*The Soulmate Experience* has quite literally given me a new way to look at my life." ~EVIE ROMERO

"A truly wonderful book: easy to read and digest, practical, lighthearted, full of compassion and encouragement. One of those books you can pick up for a few moments and transform your day." ~ED TUCKER

"You are in great hands here with Mali and Joe and *The Soulmate Experience*. Their loving hearts, minds, and souls are here to change the world as we know it." ~COLETTE KENNEY

"This book demonstrates what soul-level connection is all about and how it can be cultivated—with lots of suggestions and ways for couples to get there together." ~MONTY PERRY

"The planet needs this book as soon as possible." ~DIANE KNORR

"This is a great guide to follow if you want a soulmate relationship— not only with that special someone, but with everyone you will ever meet." ~MATTHEW M. WATSON

"Looking at conflict as an opportunity to make a deeper connection with my husband shifted my thinking and deepened my love." ~AMY ZIMMER

"Thank you for being a part of the healing of the world!" ~AVASA LOVE

"What a pleasurable book to read! The language is so natural, the stories so easy to identify with, and the advice so practical—I felt like I was sitting around a kitchen table having a conversation with the authors." ~DIANE HART

"Buy this book even if you don't think you need it. The messages in it will transform your life and your relationships." ~JEAN MARSHALL

"Mali and Joe offer inspiration and affirmation along every step of the path." ~BETH MIDDLECAMP

"No matter how many other relationship books you've read, this is *the* book that gives you the tools to attract a soulmate, and find solutions to the challenges of relationship that will allow that soulmate experience to blossom." ~JOANNE SPROTT

"Thank you for sharing your great teachings and way of being together in the world." ~SANDY MORRIS

"As a married couple, we are delighted with this book. *The Soulmate Experience* is a must-read for all those desiring to bring love to themselves and healing to the world." ~CAROLE CHRISTE AND BUZZ FOOTE

"When I think of being in the presence of you two, I am overwhelmed with love and peace. Thank you for being here and being awakened." ~MEGAN MONIQUE HARNER

"I just need to keep reading this book over and over again. It's made a huge difference in meeting new people." ~DEBORAH NEWTON

"This book is not just about creating soulmate relationships with others. It's about loving yourself enough to be open to receiving and giving love. I just want to buy up a million copies for all of my friends!" ~KATIE LE NORMAND

"Love the ideas and concepts—and especially the tons of easy to understand, practical suggestions." ~DEANNA DUDNEY

"The world is a better place because the two of you care so much." ~PAUL CONTENTO

"I love this book. Do you think it would marry me?" ~ANNA EMBREE

THE
SOULMATE
EXPERIENCE

A Practical Guide to
Creating Extraordinary Relationships

Mali Apple & Joe Dunn

San Rafael, California

Published in the United States by A Higher Possibility, San Rafael, California
www.ahigherpossibility.com

Editor: Anna Embree
Cover design: David Woods
Interior art: Freedom Bean
Author photograph: Dominic Colacchio
Michael Naumer photograph: Mary Small

Cover image, top: Copyright Serghei Velusceac, 2011. Bottom: Copyright Héctor Fernández Santos-Díez, 2011. Used under license from Shutterstock.com.

Publishers Cataloging-in-Publication Data
Apple, Mali.
   The soulmate experience : a practical guide to creating extraordinary relationships / Mali Apple , Joe Dunn.
   p.   cm.
   Includes index.
   ISBN 978-0-9845622-0-6
   1. Interpersonal relations.   2. Self-actualization (Psychology).
3. Intimacy (Psychology).   4. Love.   5. Soul mates.
I. Dunn, Joseph, 1958–. II. Title.
   HQ801.A71   2011
   646.7'7—dc22   2011901407

10 9 8 7 6 5 4 3 2 1

First Edition

To Joe

For so willingly exploring all that it means to be in love
For gently encouraging me to be everything
I have the potential to be
And most of all, for opening my heart

Mali

To Mali

My lover, my spiritual teacher, and my best friend
I will be forever grateful for this heart-opening
opportunity to live life with you

Joe

Contents

A Word About
Our Soulmate Experience

Just like many other couples in a new relationship, we experienced a deeply profound, almost magical feeling of connection, what many would call a soulmate connection. But rather than gradually fading away, as so often happens, the love and passion we were experiencing actually continued to grow. We eventually found ourselves inspired—and even compelled—to investigate just what was making this "soulmate experience" possible. *What was keeping the magic alive?*

As we dedicated ourselves and our relationship to exploring this one question, we also began to coach singles and couples in applying our discoveries so that they could transform their own lives. We're thrilled by the rapid shifts we're seeing in the people we inspire and coach. People from all over the world say they're feeling more loving and accepting toward themselves, more connected to those around them, and more confident about the possibility of creating their own soulmate experience. And many of them are doing just that.

This is not just another relationship book. Many of our ideas are unconventional. They also *work*.

People often tell us we're the happiest couple they've ever met. They see how connected we are, and they want to know our secrets. These are our "secrets"—all the ideas, tools, and techniques we use to continually create a magical life together.

We use these ideas to allow the things that come up in every relationship—from fears and expectations to jealousy and resentment—to *enhance* our experience rather than detract from it.

We use these ideas to lovingly guide each other into opening up to everything we have the potential to be.

We use these ideas to keep the love, passion, and fun alive, *every single day*.

We believe that as you incorporate even just a few of these ideas into your own life, all your relationships—including the one you have with yourself—will begin to feel more loving, more connected, and more rewarding. You'll find yourself feeling confident, excited, and inspired. And you will realize that you have everything it takes to create *your* soulmate experience.

In love,

Mali and Joe

Introduction

A re you longing for a soulmate, someone you feel deeply connected to emotionally, physically, and spiritually? Are you
ready to finally have *your* soulmate experience?

To make your dreams of such a relationship a reality, you don't
have to be one of the lucky ones. Rather than wishing or waiting for
your soulmate to show up, there are fundamental shifts you can make
right now to draw that experience into your life.

The possibilities presented in this book, and the uplifting stories of
people successfully putting them into practice, will give you the insight
and inspiration to create and sustain your own soulmate experience.

PART 1:
CREATING YOUR SOULMATE EXPERIENCE

Relationships with soulmate potential come around a lot more often
than you might imagine. The problem is, we're not always available
for them. The ideas and exercises in **Part 1: Creating Your Soulmate**

Experience are designed to help you identify and clear out anything that might be preventing you from having a deeply connected relationship. By being *available* for the soulmate experience, you will naturally *attract* it into your life.

- **Chapter 1: Changing Your Mind** presents a powerful process for identifying and "trading up" attitudes and beliefs that aren't producing the experiences you desire. You'll also learn how to change your experience when feelings like insecurity, jealousy, or anger come over you.

- **Chapter 2: Loving Your Body** will help you to quiet your self-critical voice, see yourself without judgment, and treat yourself with more compassion and appreciation. You'll discover why accepting, appreciating, and even loving the body you have right now increases your availability for the soulmate experience.

- **Chapter 3: Reducing Your Baggage** will give you simple and effective techniques for releasing feelings of loneliness, doubt, or anxiety, freeing yourself from resentment, and genuinely increasing your self-worth.

- **Chapter 4: Raising Your Soulmate Potential** will help you cultivate qualities that will make it much easier to manifest a truly connected relationship.

PART 2:
KEEPING YOUR SOULMATE EXPERIENCE ALIVE

Every bit as important as attracting your soulmate experience is creating an environment for it to thrive. **Part 2: Keeping Your Soulmate Experience Alive** will give you tools and techniques for approaching the most challenging aspects of relationships in ways that will actually bring you and your partner closer together.

- **Chapter 5: Having a Guest in Your Life** introduces the soulmate model for creating extraordinary relationships. This enlightened approach to having a partner will help you ensure that your relationship continues to be loving, vibrant, and connected.

- **Chapter 6: Creating a Context** explores how to create an intention for your relationship that will guide and support you as the relationship adapts to changing circumstances and expands in new directions.

- **Chapter 7: Making Space** will help you create a safe, loving, receptive space for your relationship that encourages both of you to share your deepest thoughts, feelings, and desires. You'll also discover how to approach changes and challenges in ways that will *increase* the love and intimacy between you.

- **Chapter 8: Turning Expectations into Invitations** explores what may be the single greatest threat to any relationship: expectation. You'll come away with an invaluable technique for transforming potentially destructive *expectations* into simple, loving *invitations*.

- **Chapter 9: Transforming the Energy of Jealousy** will show you how to harness this powerful emotion to increase the passion, appreciation, and desire in your relationship. You will also discover the profound intimacy that results from coming together to explore jealousy's underlying causes.

- **Chapter 10: Playing Leapfrog** demonstrates powerful ways for assisting each other in healing from your pasts and rising above your perceived limitations. You'll also discover how to encourage and inspire one another to unlock the potential in every area of your lives and become your very best selves.

- **Chapter 11: Exploring the Edges** shows you how to keep the mystery and excitement in your relationship alive by "playing at your edges" in ways that are both intimate and fun. You'll also learn how to energize your sexual connection by helping each other break through limiting beliefs about yourselves and your sexuality.

- **Chapter 12: Connecting on a Soul Level** presents the five simple practices at the heart of relating on a soul-to-soul level. These practices, which are the foundation for every idea in this book, have the power to make every aspect of your relationship—and your life—more joyful, rewarding, and fulfilling.

WHO THIS BOOK IS FOR

Whether you are looking for a partner or already have one, this book contains the guidance, tools, and techniques you need to create a relationship that's fully connected and alive. This book is for you whether you're on a quest for your soulmate or just want to add more "soulmate experience" to the relationship you already have.

If you're single, you will discover how to cultivate qualities that will attract the soulmate experience into your life. You'll also learn how to recognize and draw out the soulmate potential in others.

If you're with a partner who doesn't share your enthusiasm for these ideas, you'll discover how you can transform your own experience—and be happier in the relationship for as long as you choose to stay in it.

If you already happen to be with the love of your life, you will learn exciting new ways to make sure you're keeping the *life* in your *love*.

The life-changing ideas in this book—and the many examples of real people using them successfully—will guide and support you as you create your own soulmate experience: a relationship that is a continual source of love, inspiration, and joy.

IN TRIBUTE TO
MICHAEL NAUMER

Mary Small

Michael Naumer (1942–2001) was a brilliant man who devoted much of his life's energy to teaching people how to create loving, connected relationships. Joe, who had the privilege to study under him in the mid-1990s, credits Michael with helping him to vastly improve how he approaches not only his relationships but his entire life.

Michael and his wife Christina founded the Relationships Research Institute out of their shared passion for understanding what it takes to keep a relationship healthy and vital. Hundreds of people participated in their powerful, life-changing seminars.

Catherine Sevenau, Michael's assistant for the three years prior to his death, describes what it was like to take his seminar for the first time:

> The course was about transformation. It was three intense days of awakening people to their conscious and unconscious beliefs. I was rocked, inspired, pained, and touched—but most of all, my thinking

and way of seeing my relationships and myself were completely transformed. I came out of that weekend with a heightened awareness and some practical tools that forever changed me.

Michael's words live on in the hearts and minds of the people who were fortunate enough to have known him. "Love is the recognition of the equal in the other," he liked to say. "When you diminish another person, you lose their ability to contribute to you." And, "Are you available for the relationship you say you want?"

In the spirit of keeping Michael's wisdom alive, we've chosen to honor his life and teachings by presenting some of his inspiring ideas in this book. We hope you're moved to put them to use and, as Michael would have said, "transform the process of relationship from a game you can't win to one you can't lose."

Part 1

Creating Your
Soulmate Experience

The ideas and techniques that follow
will help you identify and clear out
any obstacles that might be keeping you
from *your* soulmate experience.
When you're truly available
for the soulmate experience,
you will naturally begin
to attract it into your life.

1

Changing Your Mind

Your beliefs about yourself, other people, and the world around
you have much more control over your life than you may
realize. Clearing out limiting beliefs and positions will free you
to pursue a higher purpose: creating the space for the
enlightened relationships and joyful experiences you desire.

All of her adult life, Alison has had the belief that she's unattractive. She makes an effort to wear stylish clothing and to keep a smile on her face, but wherever she goes, she feels uncomfortable about her appearance.

Alison has an identical twin, Andrea. They're such look-alikes that even their closest friends are sometimes fooled. For whatever reasons, Andrea grew up believing that she scores about average on the attractiveness scale.

The twins are both single. When they are out together, Andrea continually attracts attention from men. Even from across the room, they pick her out as the one to approach. It's as though Alison hardly exists. She's left mystified, wondering what men see in Andrea that they don't see in her.

What is it that draws people more to one sister than to the other? What gives these two women such dissimilar experiences? It's the different *beliefs* they hold about themselves, and the types of thoughts those beliefs produce.

As far back as she can remember, Alison has compared herself to other women. When she goes out, her belief that she's unattractive hovers in the background, producing a continuous stream of negative thoughts. "I wish I was pretty like that woman over there. I should have worn a dress; my thighs look too big in these jeans."

The effects of these internal conversations are easy to see. Alison's body language gives people the impression that she's uncomfortable, unhappy, or just uninterested.

When Andrea, on the other hand, has thoughts about her own attractiveness, they tend to be along the lines of "Blue looks better on me than yellow. I love how these earrings sparkle in my hair." Her positive self-talk makes her at ease with herself and quick to smile.

YOUR BELIEFS CREATE YOUR EXPERIENCE

We often treat our beliefs as though they are indisputable truths. Yet we all learned the meaning of "belief" in grade school: an idea that is held as true. The dictionary defines the word as "something that is believed." In other words, *a belief is simply an idea that we've decided is true.*

Our personal reality—or how we perceive and experience the world—is, to a great extent, formed by our beliefs. We're programmed to go out and, as Michael Naumer* used to say, "find evidence" for every belief and position we hold. If you

The quality of your experience is a direct reflection of the quality of your beliefs.

believe that someone doesn't like you, you can easily interpret their frown as evidence of that dislike, even when their expression relates to something else entirely. Because our minds are capable of quickly producing evidence for almost any belief, we can easily prove to ourselves again and again that what we believe is simply the way it is.

Long before we reach adulthood, we will have accumulated thousands of beliefs, from specific ones like "I'm not coordinated" and "Holidays are difficult for me" to larger, overarching beliefs like "The world isn't a safe place," "People are going to take advantage of me," "I'll never get what I want," and "Nobody understands me." We also develop positive beliefs, like "I love rainy weather" and "I'm good at organizing." This collection of beliefs is largely responsible for creating our personal experience. The world shows up pretty much the way we expect it to.

One Thanksgiving, Grace invited her neighbors Dave and Sandra to join her family for dinner. Dave offered to bring dessert from a local bakery, and Sandra said she'd love to make the mashed potatoes. They were both grateful for the invitation. Grace's sisters, however, were not quite so taken with the idea.

---

*See pages viii and ix for an introduction to Michael Naumer, who is quoted throughout this book.

"How can he bring a store-bought pie?" Jeanne questioned Grace. "Thanksgiving is supposed to be about *preparing* a meal. Come on; it only takes an hour to make a pie!"

"I don't want someone else's mashed potatoes," their sister Patricia added. "It wouldn't be the same."

With these beliefs, Jeanne and Patricia have set the stage for their evening. They'll show up for dinner with some measure of resistance already in place. Grace, on the other hand, with her focus on the celebration, will enjoy the pie and potatoes wherever they come from.

As another example of how our beliefs create our experience, take Greg, a thirty-something accountant who is extremely nervous about meeting new people. When he anticipates meeting someone for the first time, his heart rate and blood pressure jump. He starts to sweat. When he is finally introduced, he checks out his body's condition and concludes, "See? I hate meeting new people. Look what it does to me!"

Greg has taken his body's response to the belief "I don't like meeting new people" as *proof* that his belief is the *truth*. He associates his physical reactions with meeting someone new, rather than with the real cause: his belief and the stream of thoughts his belief generates— thoughts like "I hope Sheila doesn't try to introduce me to that woman. Why did I agree to come? I should leave now before she calls me over."

Each of us has a unique set of beliefs through which we evaluate and draw conclusions about ourselves and the world. Let's run the idea "I'd like to write a book" through three different sets of beliefs and see what comes out. One possible belief is "I don't have the education, money, or support I'd need to make that happen." Another belief might be "There are probably too many books like this out there already." A third might be "If I really have the desire to do something, I know I have what it takes to turn that desire into a reality." Now suppose these three would-be authors are all experts on a particular topic and equally talented as writers. Which one has the best chance of actually producing a book?

CHANGE YOUR BELIEFS, CHANGE YOUR EXPERIENCE

Many of us will initially resist the idea that we can intentionally and significantly alter our beliefs. This is understandable. Our families, schools, religions, and societies, as well as the media, all reinforce the notion that the beliefs we hold are more or less the truth. They remind us daily that the outside world is responsible for our internal experience. Many of our beliefs have been with us for so long that they feel like they're just part of who we are.

The truth is, *you can change what you believe*. You change your beliefs all the time in response to new information and experiences. You can probably easily identify beliefs you once held quite strongly that you no longer have, as well as beliefs you're holding now that you didn't have ten years ago.

If Alison changes her belief about herself—if she decides that although she doesn't feel particularly attractive, she's not unattractive either—don't you think she will have a different experience? If the woman who once believed "I'm unattractive" can trade up to the belief

"I'm really not so bad," she's likely to find that people are as drawn to her as they are to her sister. She'll also be pleased to discover that the improved relationship she has with herself will naturally lead to better relationships with others.

Of course, Alison has to really believe this new idea. How can she *know* that her new thought about herself is as believable as her old one? She has her sister as living proof. You may not have the benefit of a twin sister, but for any belief you hold, there's someone out there who, under very similar circumstances, holds an entirely different belief. Their belief works for them, and it can work for you.

What about Greg, the accountant? Suppose he were to recognize that his aversion to meeting new people comes from a belief he's holding. Imagine that he decides to replace the belief "I hate meeting new people" with "Meeting new people is okay." He might even remind himself that millions of people approach meeting someone new with excitement. You can be sure that if Greg tries on the belief "Meeting new people is fun," he'll have a much better time at the next company picnic.

Life shows up to match your beliefs about it.

Some people will concede that it might be possible to alter a belief here and there, but argue that many if not most of our beliefs are "hardwired" into us and therefore can't be changed. Take the idea of our needs, the things we believe we must have in order to feel happy, satisfied, or fulfilled. Our true physical needs are food, water, clothing, and shelter. We might also want to add human contact to that list. Anything else we call a need is, in reality, something we want or desire. We tell ourselves that if we don't get these "needs" met, we will experience unhappiness in some form, such as disappointment, frustration, resentment, or anger.

This applies to our values as well. What we call a value is simply a collection of related beliefs. Suzanne, for example, says she values traditional family life. What this means is that she has a set of beliefs about what is right and proper when it comes to families: "Families should make an effort to eat dinner together several nights a week." "People should raise children to respect their elders." "My sister should be supportive when she knows I'm going through a difficult time." Suzanne could have hundreds of beliefs related to this one value. Someone else could have an entirely different set of beliefs around the same value. Like our beliefs, our values are not permanent fixtures: They evolve as we do. Some people's values change in only small ways over their lifetime, while other people have transformational experiences that can shift their entire value system in an instant.

Like puppets, we often find ourselves being controlled by our beliefs with no awareness of who is really pulling the strings. Until we can look in the mirror and become acquainted with our puppeteer, many of us will continue to feel pushed around, physically and emotionally. We will continue to put the blame on our circumstances, the people around us, and the world in general rather than where it belongs: on our own set of beliefs, through which we interpret everything that happens to us.

Your beliefs create your experience. If a belief you have isn't bringing you the experience you desire, you have three choices. You can continue to feel disappointed and resentful every time life doesn't live up to your belief. You can trade up, replacing your belief with one that has a better chance of bringing you what you want. Or you can let go of your belief altogether and choose to accept life exactly as it shows up.

Get this one idea down—that your beliefs create your experience and that what you believe is up to you—and life will begin to flow much more easily.

If you've faced traumatic experiences or difficult circumstances in your life, such as abuse or extreme hardship, this concept may not seem immediately useful to you. However, transforming the way you *relate* to your memories—without condoning anyone's abusive actions—can make a significant contribution to your healing process.

CORE BELIEFS

Core beliefs are firmly embedded beliefs with far-reaching implications about who we are. Generally with us from our earliest years, our core beliefs are hugely influential forces. Consider what kinds of experiences these core beliefs would produce:

- "I'm not good enough."
- "I'm unlovable."
- "I don't fit in."
- "The world's a scary place."
- "People will take advantage of me whenever they can."
- "I'll never get what I want."

Walter, an insurance agent, identifies his most influential core belief as "There's not enough." This core belief affects every facet of his life. At work, he's nervous that the new saleswoman will take away his accounts because there won't be enough customers for them both. He thinks if he asks for an ergonomic chair to replace the one that's giving him constant back pain, he'll be seen as wasting company resources and will be passed over for a promotion. Why? *Because there's not enough.* Walter is reluctant to donate to charity, do favors for people, or even let friends borrow books. *If there's not enough— money, time, energy—there's not enough to give.* Although he much prefers the atmosphere and food at his favorite restaurant, he usually ends up at the cafe across the street because dinners there cost two dollars less. Whenever conversations with his wife turn to their saving or retirement plans, they end up in an argument. Why? *Because there's just not enough!*

Anna is a stay-at-home mother of two. One of her most influential core beliefs, "I should be perfect," has affected every aspect of her life. Practically every relationship, experience, and decision has been influenced by it to some degree. It has generated thousands of thoughts over the thirty or so years it's been in operation and has been the source of anxiety, worry, stress, guilt, frustration, and even moments of self-hatred. With this belief holding such a position of power in her life, it was impossible for Anna to ever feel fully comfortable, even when

> **A core belief is always operating behind the scenes. The trick is to take a peek backstage.**
>
>

she was alone. She always had a nagging feeling that whatever she was doing simply wasn't good enough. Once she finally identified this core belief and began watching for its influence, she realized it was operating in the background all day long.

Of course, we might also have positive core beliefs. Ellen, for example, has always had the belief "I'm lovable." She says, "Even when I'm not at my best, I accept that as just part of being human. I'm still lovable!"

Uncovering a negative core belief will begin to transform your life. Every time you become aware of how your belief is affecting you, it will reduce its grip on you. Although you are unlikely to dissolve a core belief all at once, as you continue to expose it, its influence over you will lessen.

HOW YOUR BELIEFS
AFFECT YOUR RELATIONSHIPS

What does what you believe have to do with the soulmate experience? It's difficult to have an extraordinary relationship when your mind is cluttered with less-than-extraordinary beliefs. If you believe in lack, you'll see lack wherever you look. If you believe in abundance, you'll see abundance. Although it's possible to have a relationship with any set of beliefs, every limiting belief and inflexible position we hold will reduce our potential for a soulmate experience.

Changing or letting go of beliefs and positions that aren't working for you will go a long way toward making you available for the enlightened relationship you desire. This is true both before you enter a relationship and when you're in one.

The people we attract into our lives reflect the beliefs we hold about ourselves.

First, raising the quality of the beliefs you hold about yourself will automatically raise your sense of self-worth. This is especially important to understand before you get into a new relationship. People with low self-worth tend to attract partners who also have low self-worth—and possibly even partners who will eventually turn to abusive behavior in order to try to feel in control. The more you raise your self-worth, the higher the quality of the potential partners you will attract.

Second, when you're in a relationship, having flexibility about what you believe will be very useful when it comes to keeping your relationship vibrant and alive. Learning how to change or let go of your beliefs when they aren't serving you and your relationship will enable you to respond fluidly to—and make the most of—the challenges you are bound to encounter.

Many of our beliefs directly affect our ability to form and maintain healthy, rewarding intimate relationships. Consider these:

- "Women are never satisfied."
- "Men aren't emotionally available."
- "Women aren't reliable."
- "Men can't be trusted."
- "There's no one I'm really compatible with."

What are the chances of having a truly connected experience with another human being if we go around with beliefs like these? As Michael Naumer put it, "If you believe men are jerks, it's amazing how many jerks you will attract! And you'll be able to gather overwhelming evidence for how men are jerks. 'You're just like the rest of them,' you'll say. 'I knew it all along.'" In fact, one way to identify your core beliefs about relationships is to look at the similarities among the relationships you've had in the past.

BE YOUR OWN WITNESS

Our beliefs produce a continuous stream of thoughts from morning to night. You might be surprised by the variety and number of thoughts that a particular belief can generate. For example, suppose you go through the day with the belief "There's not enough time to get everything done." Your mind will keep itself occupied producing evidence for this belief, and you might find yourself with thoughts like, "Why can't the light be green this one time? Look at that parking lot—is everyone in town shopping here? The sign clearly says ten items or less; that woman must have twenty things in her cart. How am I going to drop off the cleaning in time to pick up the kids?" Sound familiar?

This particular line of thinking is likely to make you feel anxious, irritable, and possibly overwhelmed. Though we tend to associate our emotional responses with the events or circumstances in our lives—like the crowded parking lot and the woman ahead of us in line—*the true cause of our emotional response to an event is the thoughts we have about that event.* Our body translates our thoughts into chemical and physical responses that we experience as emotions. In other words, *emotions are the body's response to the thoughts we think.*

Learn to pay attention to your thoughts and the emotions that they produce. *Being the witness,* as this is called, requires focus and intention. As with any skill, it grows much easier with practice.

Emotions like anger, jealousy, and insecurity are an indication that you're resisting "what is." These emotions are often pointing to a belief you have about how things should be that contradicts the way they really are. As soon as possible after such a feeling arises, examine it to discover the thought or thoughts that generated it.

Feelings like jealousy and anger can come up so quickly that it can be difficult to cycle back and pinpoint the thoughts behind them. As you practice this skill, though, the interval between the onset of an emotion and your awareness of it will lessen, and identifying the underlying belief will become easier. In time you will learn to "catch" your emotions as they arise, bringing your awareness to them soon after they are triggered and looking beyond them to the generating thoughts. Even if those thoughts were subtle or fleeting and you're tempted to conclude that the emotions arose all on their own, if you're persistent, you will uncover the thoughts responsible for them.

As you develop the habit of being the witness to your thoughts and your emotional responses to them, the direct relationship between your beliefs and your experience will become much more

obvious. By gaining perspective of
yourself as the true creator of your
personal reality, you will also see that
you are never really a victim of your
circumstances. Although it's true you
have little control over most of what

> **A powerful question
> to ask yourself is,**
> *Is this belief bringing me
> the experience I desire?*

happens in the world, you have tremendous influence over your *experience* of the events and circumstances of your life. When you can really grasp this idea, life becomes much less of a struggle.

In this way, being the witness to your internal experience will, on its own, bring more harmony into your life. In addition, once you develop the awareness to be able to point to a belief and say, "This is simply an idea I'm choosing to interpret my experience through, and it isn't working very well for me," you have the opportunity to transform your experience. You can create a new experience by trying on a new belief, or even letting go of your belief entirely.

TRANSFORM YOUR LIMITING BELIEFS

People are drawn to the soulmate experience in part because of the freedom, joy, and connection it offers, but these positive states are largely unavailable to us when our minds are churning out thoughts that fill us with dissatisfaction, fear, frustration, and resentment. Knowing how to transform your limiting beliefs and inflexible positions into beliefs that support you rather than cripple you will help you attract the quality of relationship you desire. Even if you're working through past trauma or abuse, this knowledge will make an important contribution to your overall healing process.

You can use the following four-step technique to upgrade any belief that's not bringing you the experience you'd like. This might require you to release long-ingrained habits or give up your urge to be right. Be assured that as you practice the art of upgrading your beliefs, it will grow easier. And the results will inspire you to continue identifying and transforming the beliefs that aren't serving you.

Once you've reviewed this process for transforming your limiting beliefs, remember to come back and use it!

Step 1: Identify the Belief

Your first clue that you have a limiting belief operating will often be a separating emotion like anxiety, anger, or jealousy. Separating emotions are those that make us feel *separate* from other people rather than *connected* to them. When you feel one of these emotions, train yourself to trace it back to the thought or thoughts that preceded it. Sometimes it will be obvious what those thoughts are. At other times, your thoughts may have been so subtle or fleeting that identifying them will require some focused investigation.

When you recognize that you're experiencing a separating emotion, *resist the temptation to let it direct your words or actions.* Not acting when you're under the influence of a separating emotion can be challenging, but it creates space for you to explore what's really going on. As soon as possible, put your full attention on the feeling of the emotion in your body. If circumstances require you to wait before you do this, reproduce the emotion later by mentally re-creating the situation it came up in.

Stay with the feeling for a while, listening for the thoughts going on in the background. Write your thoughts down as you uncover them. Don't allow yourself to indulge in them; just get them down on paper. If you feel you just can't find the thoughts associated with the emotion, simply imagine what thoughts *could* have produced it. You can work with these ideas just as effectively.

When you feel you've recorded all the thoughts you can find in yourself that are related to this incident, take a good, long look at them. Then, as clearly as you can, put into words the belief responsible for producing them. This will be a short, concise statement, such as "I didn't go to college, so I have nothing of value to contribute." "My family should understand me." "I'm not pretty enough." It may take you a few tries to get a clear, accurate statement of your belief.

Once you've written this belief down, check that it could indeed have been responsible for producing all the thoughts on your list.

Step 2: Examine the Belief

Think back to other times and situations when this belief has been operating, and add to your list any additional thoughts it has been responsible for. It may well have been influencing you for years.

When your list is complete, slowly read through it again. Focus your attention on the emotions that come up as you repeat each thought to yourself. As you experience the effects of these emotions in your body, remind yourself that your emotions are directly related to your thoughts rather than to what's happening in the outside world.

Now it's time to assess the impact the belief has had on your life. Ask yourself these questions: *In what ways has this belief prevented me from feeling at ease in the world? How has it limited my ability to connect with other people? How would my experience be different if I were free from this belief?*

Suppose you identify your belief as "My family should understand me." This belief has probably made you feel apprehensive, irritable, and resentful whenever you and your family spend time together. It's certainly made it more difficult to connect with them. If you were to give up the belief that your family should understand you, you'd find it much easier to enjoy your time with them—whether they happen to understand you or not.

Step 3: Craft a Replacement Belief

By making a thorough assessment of the harmful effects your belief has had on your life, you may already begin to feel its influence diminish. In fact, sometimes the damage a belief is causing is so clear, and your desire to end your suffering so strong, that you can simply drop the belief right then and there.

If you can't let go of your belief completely, you can always trade up. Craft a replacement belief that you can use to replace your old belief every time it shows up.

While focusing on the belief you've identified, search for another idea you hold—one you may not have put into words before—that would produce *positive* thoughts instead of negative thoughts in these same circumstances. This replacement belief will be an idea that comes from a place of love rather than from a place of fear—an idea that embraces rather than rejects "what is." This is not a statement of something you *wish* were true. *An effective replacement belief is an idea you accept as every bit as valid as your original belief.*

Suppose you recognize that you have the belief "I'm not talented enough to succeed in this field." Your replacement belief could be "I'm so passionate about this field that I'll learn all I need to succeed." If your original belief is "My family should understand me," your replacement belief might be "My family is doing the best they know how." If your original belief is "I'm not pretty enough," you might recognize that "I feel pretty when I allow myself to really connect with others" is just as true. Make your replacement statement as clear and simple as you can. If it's too complex, it may be hard to recall when you're under the influence of powerful emotions.

Now take yourself back to each of the situations you identified in which your old belief was operating. Spend some time imagining what your experience would be like with your new belief in play instead. How would you feel? What would you do or say?

Step 4: Reprogram Your Old Belief

Now every time you experience a separating emotion and trace it back to some variation of your old belief, train yourself to refocus your attention on your new belief instead. Because the new belief is just as true for you, simply shifting your focus to your new belief will immediately begin to transform your experience.

Which belief will bring you the quality of experience you desire: your old one or your new one?

It can take considerable willpower to maintain the self-awareness necessary for this practice, so it's helpful to post your replacement belief where you will see it regularly. You can even repeat it to yourself as a mantra when you find yourself in the grip of strong emotions.

Feel the truth of your new belief every time you use it. Find a place inside yourself and in your experience where it is true for you. In addition, remember that your mind will dutifully gather evidence for the beliefs you hold. So direct your mind to find evidence for your new belief, both now and in your past experiences.

The process of catching your old belief in operation and replacing it with your new one will grow easier over time. As you continue to remind yourself of your new belief, you will experience a tremendous increase in your ability to feel connected to other people and comfortable in the world.

REPROGRAMMING IN OPERATION

Let's suppose you're waiting in line at the grocery store and begin to feel impatient and irritated. Once you realize you're having these emotions, you might scan back through your recent internal dialogue and recognize that you've been telling yourself, "That cashier should stop chatting and focus on moving the line along. They should have more checkers at this time of day."

You could then try to identify the belief underlying these thoughts and put it into words: "Cashiers should be efficient." You might also phrase it as "People shouldn't waste time when there's a line" or "People should focus on doing their jobs." The precise wording isn't important. Working with any of these statements will help free you from the real source of your irritation: your idea that something should be different from the way it is.

When you assess the impact this belief has had on your life, you might realize that you've been sabotaging your ability to enjoy the present moment and, for example, to possibly make a connection with the person behind you in line. If you reprogrammed your belief with "It's great when people are efficient," which you might find just as believable, you'd probably have a better experience standing in lines. This belief would cause you to notice when people *are* being efficient rather than when they aren't. It may even move you to compliment cashiers who are able to handle pressure with grace. If you do choose to act—speaking with the manager about the long lines, for example—you'll do so with a positive attitude, which will make you far more effective.

Melissa, a part-time writing teacher, often found herself obsessing about her boyfriend: his whereabouts, his long-term plans, and when he would next email or call her. These constant thoughts kept her feeling anxious and ungrounded, and they had been the cause of several disagreements.

Melissa spent some time taking a look at all the thoughts she had around this issue and traced them back to the core belief "There's not enough love for me." She easily identified other situations where this belief had influenced her thinking, such as with her family, her friends, and even her students. She could see how the low-level anxiety and fear these thoughts produced prevented her from being fully present with what she was doing or who she was with.

When she turned her attention to crafting a replacement belief, it occurred to her that many of these same people often told her how inspirational she was. She realized that she was so overflowing with love herself that she had more than enough love with which to inspire others. These days, when-ever she detects the belief "There's not enough love for me" operating, she practices refocusing her attention on the belief "I'm so overflowing with love that I inspire others" and feels an immediate surge in self-confidence.

> Reprogramming long-ingrained habits can only be done with *practice*.

Josie, a musician and artist, spends much of the year traveling and has friends all over the world. Many of her friends are involved in fascinating projects and work with famous and talented people. Josie is inspired by her friends and the great work they're doing, but she also admits she sometimes finds herself feeling inadequate and left out when she's around them.

When she investigated the source of these feelings, Josie realized that she'd been operating under the belief "I'm not interesting." This belief expresses itself through thoughts that she isn't as dynamic or intriguing as other people in her life—thoughts that leave her feeling disconnected and unappreciated. In trying to craft a replacement belief, it occurred to Josie that she must be at least *somewhat* interesting to attract so many talented and fascinating people into her life! She could see that the belief "I am interesting" really could be as true for her as her original belief.

Cole, a real estate agent, occasionally finds himself feeling uncomfortable when he is in the presence of people with more education than he has. This feeling is particularly strong when he's asked for his opinion on subjects he knows little about, like politics or technology. After looking at the thoughts that produce this feeling—thoughts like "They're going to think I'm not very educated" and "I'm not much help in this area"—Cole phrased the belief responsible for them as "I didn't go to college, so I have nothing of value to contribute."

When Cole looked more deeply into the truth of whether he actually does have anything of value to offer, he realized that his lack of knowledge about any particular topic actually gives him an advantage: He can frequently see things from a broader perspective when others are getting lost in the details. Cole phrased his replacement belief as "I can contribute my ability to see the big picture." He can easily find evidence in past experiences for how valuable his ability to see the bigger picture actually is.

When he uses his new belief, Cole reports that it instantly expands his perspective on the topic at hand. In addition to giving him something to contribute, the new belief allows him to feel much more relaxed and engaged with the people around him.

Sometimes we're able to simply drop a belief altogether when we see it's not serving us. Galen, a motorcycle mechanic and handyman, got up one morning and tripped over his sleeping cat. At breakfast, he spilled coffee on the clean shirt he'd just put on. Once he'd changed clothes, he headed toward the door and realized he'd misplaced his car keys. At this point he mumbled aloud to himself, "It's gonna be one of those days."

Galen's first errand of the morning was to stop by the hardware store. When he got there, he looked around at the full parking lot; every spot was taken. He was about to add the lack of a parking space to his list of complaints when he suddenly realized that with his belief "It's going to be one of those days," he had set himself up to find evidence for what was "wrong" all day long.

At that moment, Galen looked back at his morning and realized that he actually had much to be grateful for: He had a warm, safe bed to sleep in; he could afford coffee and a car; he had good friends, an affectionate cat, and a life that he loved. And he said to himself, "This is going to be a great day."

You now have a powerful tool you can use to transform your experience every time you find yourself being influenced by a negative emotion or thought pattern. By learning how to free yourself from limiting beliefs and the emotions that accompany them, you'll be much more available for an authentic, connected relationship.

2

Loving Your Body

Too many of us go through life feeling less than loving toward our
own bodies. We believe we're not attractive enough, not fit enough,
or just flawed in one way or another. Such a negative self-image
prevents us from fully sharing ourselves and can severely limit our
ability to be intimate. Learning to accept, appreciate, and even
love every aspect of your physical self will free you to explore new
dimensions in your life and enjoy richer, more intimate relationships.

Our perfection-obsessed culture encourages us to view our bodies as a collection of parts and then to continually identify and reject "imperfections" in those parts. If you're like many people, you have a body part—or maybe several—that you've been giving yourself negative messages about for years.

Jessica, who runs marathons in addition to raising two children and managing her own business, focuses daily on the appearance of her stomach, which remains soft and round no matter how many miles she runs or sit-ups she does. Jason checks his bald spot in the mirror almost every time he uses the restroom. Steven has worried since puberty about the size of his penis.

Self-criticism has direct effects on our intimate relationships. Although Jessica is extremely fit, her almost obsessive thoughts about her stomach keep her from being fully comfortable when she's naked. This makes sex with her husband much less enjoyable than it could be. "He tells me I'm beautiful," she says, "but when we're making love, I'm constantly distracted because I'm thinking about my stomach." Jason began going bald in his early twenties and has never been comfortable when women touch his hair. Steven, consumed with the belief that he can't satisfy a woman through intercourse, admits, "I have never found myself lost in the experience of making love. I am always too busy worrying that I won't satisfy her."

When the world around us holds up flat stomachs, full heads of hair, and large penises as models of perfection, it's easy to fall into the trap of comparing ourselves to those ideals day after day and coming up short every time. But even if we were able to "fix" the things we're convinced are our worst features—if Jessica endures liposuction, for example, or Jason goes through the pain and expense of hair implants—we wouldn't suddenly feel whole. That's because by the time we're young adults, the habit of scanning our bodies for features that don't measure up is deeply ingrained.

> **We sabotage our self-image when we mentally dissect ourselves and find fault with the individual pieces.**

The truth is, our bodies are nothing short of miraculous. For all they are and everything they do for us, they deserve our compassion, admiration, and even reverence. Yet making critical remarks about our bodies often passes for casual conversation: "These jeans make me look fat." "Trash those pictures before someone sees them. I look so old!" Even if we never criticize our bodies out loud, many of us do so daily in our heads: "I hate that double chin!" "Why did I have to get the curly hair?"

Any way in which you reject yourself prevents you from being able to fully connect with another human being. When you carry a belief that any part of you is unacceptable, you simply can't be completely present with someone else or, for that matter, even with yourself. Even if you don't belittle your body or put yourself down for not changing it in ways you would like, the more you can raise your appreciation for the body you have right now, the more available you will be for the soulmate experience.

QUIET YOUR SELF-CRITICAL VOICE

When we meet someone who has a trait that could be seen as undesirable, such as a birthmark, we don't typically start right in with criticism: "That mark on your face is so ugly. Have you considered doing something about that?"

Many of us, though, talk to ourselves regularly with just such a lack of compassion and love. Whenever we catch a glimpse of our reflection, the uncaring words are often right behind: "My skin looks splotchy." "My arms are so flabby!" "Yep, my nose is as big as it was yesterday."

If you're one of the millions of people who give themselves negative messages whenever they see themselves in a photo or the mirror, it's high time you quieted that self-critical voice.

> A steady diet of self-criticism will make even the most poised among us feel less confident, less capable, and potentially miserable.

See the Harm You've Been Doing

Though we all know that putting ourselves down will never contribute to our sense of self-worth and probably won't motivate us to take better care of our bodies, many of us can't seem to stop. One powerful first step to ending the self-criticism is to get a sense of how cruel and insensitive you've been.

Stand in front of a mirror and make an honest review of the negative messages you've been giving yourself. Do your best to recall every self-critical remark you've made in the past week or month, and say them out loud with as much sincerity as you can muster. When you've done your best to uncover them all, ask yourself these questions: *What has this self-criticism done for me? Do I deserve to be put down like this? Is this behavior likely to contribute to my health and happiness? Is this behavior making me available for the kind of relationships I'd like?*

Natalie, a mother of three young children, has regularly criticized her body ever since she gave birth to her first baby. "I'd tell myself my hips were too wide, my chest was too flat, my skin wasn't tight like it should be. Doing this before going out on a date with my husband would put me in a pretty sour mood—so much so that sometimes I couldn't even bring myself to go."

When the impact of what she'd been doing to herself hit her, Natalie said it was an incredible wake-up call. "I realized what a waste of precious time beating myself up was!" Natalie also saw that she was unintentionally modeling for her children behavior that was, in essence, self-abusive. "I decided I would do my best to start accepting that this is who I am right now and enjoying what I have."

Imagine how it would be to feel love and compassion for your miraculous body every time you looked in the mirror. This experience is within your reach—whether or not you change a single thing about your body. The realization you need is this: *Negative self-talk does you absolutely no good. More than that, it's extremely damaging to both you and your relationships.* Abusing your body, mentally or physically, is a waste of your life and the precious time you have to enjoy it. These ideas apply not only to your body, but to *anything* you don't accept about yourself: your past, your upbringing, your personality traits, or the choices you've made.

> The little things you can't accept about yourself have more control over your life than you realize.

If you've been your own worst enemy for years, make this promise to yourself right now: *From this day forward, I promise to do my best to stop the self-criticism and to love the person who's looking back at me in the mirror.* It's unlikely you'll be able to let go of your negative self-talk all at once, but it is possible to drop a substantial amount of it by becoming aware of how truly pointless and harmful it is.

Talk to Yourself with Compassion

Now that you've taken a look at all the demeaning things you tend to say to yourself, use the techniques in Chapter 1 to identify and transform the beliefs that are generating your self-defeating thoughts. You might find that deep down, you hold beliefs like "No one wants a woman with real curves" or "If I don't look like I did in my twenties, I'm not attractive."

Because our self-critical voice can be so tenacious, affirmations can help us transform how we speak to ourselves. Affirmations are positive statements, such as "I am beautiful and capable," that we can repeat to ourselves whenever our self-critical mechanism is triggered.

> Learning to love your body will raise your self-worth, which will help you attract a partner with high self-worth.

Affirmations are most effective if they are beliefs we're ready to accept as true. Jessica, the marathon runner who criticizes her stomach on a daily basis, says that repeating statements like "My belly is beautiful" or "My stomach is perfect just as it is" simply didn't work for her. "Every time I said them, I'd find myself arguing with them." Instead, she came up with this statement: "I am strong, healthy, and sexy." Because she really believes each of these ideas, this affirmation is effective for her. Now when she catches herself focusing negatively on her stomach, she quiets the self-deprecating voice by saying to herself, "I am strong, healthy, and sexy," feeling the truth in every word.

"As soon as I do that," she reports, "I immediately feel better."

Steven, who's still in the process of accepting the size of his penis, uses affirmations to remind himself of the positive things that being smaller has brought him. "I learned early on to focus on other ways to bring a woman pleasure, and I do think I'm a better lover today because of that," he says. "So when I start obsessing about my size, I remind myself that I'm a more attentive lover than I would have been."

LOOK IN THE MIRROR
AND SEE THE MIRACLE

Some of us are so used to criticizing our reflection that we haven't seen ourselves without the filter of our negative assessments in a long time. Our self-perception can be quite distorted, meaning that what we see in the mirror can be very different from what everyone else sees. Many of the features we zero in on are things nobody else would ever notice unless we pointed them out. Leslie, a cosmetologist, says she sometimes feels guilty taking people's money for certain procedures. "They're asking me to cover up spots or remove hairs I know no one else will ever see."

Michaela is a raven-haired beauty with rich brown eyes, full lips, and coffee-colored skin. Vivacious and energetic, she turns heads everywhere she goes. When she steps out of the shower and sees her reflection in the mirror, however, her attention is instantly drawn to the lines around her eyes. Though she does find

> Don't wait until ten or twenty years from now to realize you're beautiful today.

herself attractive overall, those lines are often all she sees. If anyone else happened to catch a glimpse of Michaela naked, they would see a beautiful woman with a brilliant smile, lovely skin, and strong legs. They certainly wouldn't focus in on her age lines!

If you've spent years comparing yourself to perfect, airbrushed models or beating yourself up day after day for whatever you've decided is unsatisfactory, the exercise that follows will help you begin to heal some of that self-inflicted damage.

For this exercise, set aside some time to be alone, maybe an hour or more. Have a couple of mirrors handy so that you'll be able to view yourself from various angles. As you'll be undressed at least part of the time, make sure the room is warm.

Appreciate Every Part

The first part of this practice is to find some way to appreciate every aspect of your body. Even if you feel you already accept your body as it is, this exercise will help you love yourself even more.

Begin with whatever feels natural, such as a hand, a foot, or your eyes. Focus your full attention on that one part of your body, investigating it as though you were seeing it for the first time. For instance, if you start with your hand, you might feel the texture of the skin, the smoothness of the nails, and the structure of the bones underneath. Then experiment with all the different ways your hand can move. If negative thoughts come

> When we embrace something we've rejected about ourselves, we'll naturally be more accepting of others as well.

up, allow them to drift by, without following or holding onto them, and refocus on what you appreciate.

As you connect with your hand, think about all that it's done for you. Imagine how your life would be without it. Contemplate the hundreds of thousands of tasks your hand has performed and the variety of wonderful and interesting things you've touched with it. Feel compassion for everything this body part has gone through: injuries, traumas, or even neglect.

Take a moment to honor any aspects of your hand that you may have criticized or rejected at one time or another. For instance, if you've ever thought of the veins on the backs of your hands as unattractive, contemplate how they've been there to faithfully carry blood all these years. Know that this part of you has always done the best it could.

Before moving on, find some way to feel even a small amount of gratitude for how this body part has contributed to your life. Jessica, the runner who has difficulty accepting her soft belly, might remind herself that it provided protection for her unborn babies. Steven, who has always felt less than positive about his penis, could contemplate the fact that it has provided him with a lot of pleasure over the years, as well as enabling him to father two beautiful children. Although Jason might not be able to find a way to appreciate his bald spot directly, he could focus on feeling grateful for the hair he does have.

> There's a way to appreciate every single aspect of ourselves. We just have to discover it.

Don't rush through this exercise. Make sure you go over your entire body, spending more time with those areas that have endured the most rejection.

When you finally see yourself without a filter of self-judgment, you'll look completely different!

Megan, a communications manager for an online community, found this exercise so healing that she extended it. For thirty days, she spent some time each day honoring a particular part of her body, focusing on a different part each day. This gave her the opportunity to pay attention to how she treated and thought about that part, and to find ways to honor it.

Really See Yourself—Without Self-Criticism

If you have been viewing yourself through a smokescreen of self-judgment, you've been seeing a distorted picture of who you really are. So, after getting in touch with your gratitude for the individual parts of your body, take a step back to appreciate how they all come together and contribute to this unique human being—you. For this exercise, you'll need a full-length mirror and a few candles or a room that is equipped with lights that dim. You may want to do this exercise first with your clothes on, and then undressed.

Stand in front of the mirror. Begin with a single candle or with the lights dimmed so that you can just barely perceive your outline. Your goal is to see your entire image, without focusing on any one part and without making any self-critical assessments, even if only for a few moments at a time. It may help to imagine that you are viewing your reflection from the perspective of an impartial observer, someone who has no judgment about you whatsoever. When you're able to look at yourself without judgment or criticism, gradually increase the lighting.

As you observe your reflection, feel yourself from the inside by focusing your attention on all the sensations you're experiencing. Follow each breath as it travels in and out of your body. Notice the feeling of the air on your skin. Try to detect your heartbeat and even the feeling of the blood circulating in your hands or feet. If negative thoughts arise as you observe yourself, set them aside and refocus your attention on the physical sensations you're feeling.

Appreciation Is an Ongoing Process

If you're still finding it difficult to stop criticizing a particular aspect of your body, take a little time to train yourself to redirect where your attention goes when you see your reflection. For example, if you can't seem to stop making negative comments about your teeth, learn to consciously redirect your attention to a feature you do like, such as your eyes.

It can also be helpful to try to take in the whole you—who you are beyond your physical appearance. As Deanna, a jewelry designer, says, "I like to think of myself as the 'whole' being—body/mind/ soul all interconnected—and focus on my strengths, like intelligence and creativity. If I put positive energy and thoughts into the things I like, whether it's physical or mental, it's naturally more difficult to self-criticize."

When you look in a mirror, take a moment to appreciate your favorite features.

37

Accepting your body is an ongoing process—one that will continue for as long as you have it. And the kinds of exercises described above can be extremely powerful when done with a willing partner, as you'll see later on in this book.

KNOW YOURSELF AS
ONE POSSIBLE WAY OF BEING BEAUTIFUL

Our culture defines attractiveness so narrowly that it makes it impossible for the vast majority of people to ever measure up. Rather than taking society's word for what is beautiful, discover for yourself what's beautiful—and redefine what attractive means to you.

When Ryland was nineteen, he began to grow chest hair—dark chest hair. At first he plucked the hairs that were growing beyond what he felt were acceptable boundaries. He hoped the hair would soon stop spreading, but he found his chest just wouldn't cooperate.

By the time he was twenty-one, Ryland was tired of feeling uncomfortable whenever he took his shirt off. He was tired of the demeaning remarks he'd make about himself whenever he saw his chest in the mirror: "I hate how that looks!" So he began to look for a way to be able to see himself and his chest as attractive—and he discovered Nicolas Cage. He heard women talking about how this man with dark chest hair was sexy and attractive. Ryland decided to make Nicolas Cage his "new reference point" and to choose "to reside inside this collective agreement that men who look like this are beautiful." In other words, from now on he would see himself as belonging to a group of men with a particular type of male beauty that thousands of women find attractive.

Ryland's idea of finding a new reference point can help many of us embrace our own unique form of beauty. If we feel we can't be beautiful because of particular characteristics, we can seek out new role models who we or others find attractive and who also have those traits.

For example, if you have difficulty seeing yourself as beautiful because you weigh more than you would like, you'll find plenty of heavier people who radiate confidence and beauty. Turn to these people as role models. You might also seek out the numerous websites that celebrate the beauty of all shapes and sizes, as well as inspirational television shows that help people make breakthroughs in accepting, embracing, and feeling confident in their bodies no matter what their age, shape, or size. The most important thing you can do toward making sustainable changes is to learn to love and honor your body exactly as it is right now.

> The more you love yourself, the more available you will be to love someone else.

Another step you can take toward self-acceptance is to find a way to honor what you've been rejecting. Emma spent years trying to hide her hands, believing they were too large; today she has a collection of beautiful rings to wear in celebration of all that her hands do for her. Keisha had her belly button pierced and now wears a diamond in her navel to remind her to appreciate her stomach. Christine, a mother of two who's heavier than she'd like to be, indulges in sexy bras and underwear to honor herself as a beautiful woman. Rachel named her new dog "Belly" as an ever-present reminder to love and accept her own belly.

> Go easy on yourself. Move in the direction of greater self-acceptance, while at the same time honoring where you are right now.

Knowing yourself as beautiful is entirely a matter of perspective. It's not about being a particular age, weight, or body type, having certain features, or wearing the right clothes.

When you're feeling self-critical about your appearance, remind yourself: *Who I am right now is one possible way of being beautiful.* You may be surprised to discover that the more you know yourself as beautiful, the more beauty others will see in you as well.

TUNE IN TO YOUR BODY

Imagine that a thirsty child comes to you asking for a drink and you refuse to give it to her. This may seem inconceivable, but it's not unlike how many of us—being too busy, too lazy, or simply inattentive—ignore similar requests from our own bodies every day. "Hey, aren't you listening? I'm really parched! And I've been hunched over here for hours. When do I get to stretch?" We'd be more relaxed and efficient if we learned to listen for and respond to the signs that tell us when our bodies could use food, water, exercise, or rest. We'd also be healthier, happier, and more available for creating fulfilling relationships.

Our bodies have an incredible ability to process information and are virtually self-regulating. They instinctively know whether the choices we're making about when, what, and how much to eat are healthy and nourishing. But who among us hasn't denied their body's requests for food and water or ignored the cues that they've had enough to eat?

Many of us tend to eat impulsively, letting our eyes or taste buds make our nutritional choices for us. Or we eat sporadically, ignoring the signals that we're hungry until it's too late to make a well-considered choice. If you recognize yourself here, learn to regularly check in with your body and listen to what it's telling you.

When your body says, "I don't want another bite of cake," put down your fork!

Paul, whose parents always made him eat everything on his plate, says he's learned to stop eating before he feels full. "I realized that the pressure I felt to finish a meal was imagined," he explains.

Orann, who cooks in a vegan restaurant, says he's become much more aware of how various foods affect his body. "I still eat just about anything. But now I notice that when I have a burger, thirty minutes later I feel sluggish. When I eat the food from my restaurant, I feel *awake*." By making more nutritious food choices, you nourish not only your body, but every aspect of who you are.

Our bodies also let us know whether they're getting enough exercise. Ignoring those signals leaves us feeling weak, fatigued, irritable, or even depressed. In part, that's because regular exercise rewards us with, among other things, endorphins. Released into our bodies during sustained physical activity, these "feel-good" hormones reduce anxiety and stress, decrease the experience of pain, lower blood pressure, strengthen the immune system, improve the memory, and slow the aging process. When you read that list, isn't it obvious that our bodies were meant to be nourished with endorphins on a regular basis? If all these benefits weren't enough, regular exercise can slow down the loss of muscle and bone that occurs as we age. Staying flexible through yoga or stretching helps relieve pain, improve circulation, and maintain mobility. Anything that helps reconnect us with our bodies—massage, acupuncture, warm baths, hot tubs, saunas, or just going for a walk into whatever nature is available to us—will help us tune in to our physical state.

Our bodies' need for rest is another request we frequently ignore. Even if we do manage to get enough sleep, many of us go through our days in a state of perpetual hurry, rarely ceasing our physical or mental activity to relax and recharge, even for a few minutes. We would do well to take a lesson from cats, who naturally relax all the parts of their bodies they're not using at the moment. Whatever we're doing—working at the computer, having dinner with friends, or going for a run—we can make it a habit to relax those muscles in our bodies that aren't required for that activity. Make a quick scan of your body from time to time, consciously releasing the tension in any muscles that aren't in use. You might be surprised to find your shoulders dropping several inches!

Bringing your conscious awareness to your body is a practice that will raise your appreciation for your physical self

Shift your focus from how you *look* on the outside to how you *feel* on the inside.

and make you more responsive to its signals. If you're walking, for example, tune in to all of your sense perceptions: the movement of your body, the feeling of your clothing and the air on your skin, your breathing, the sounds and sights around you. Also pay attention to internal sensations, such as the weight being transferred from one foot to the other and all the muscles that are working together to keep you balanced.

Learning to feel yourself as a whole, from the inside, may be the most precious gift you can give your body. In addition to encouraging you to make conscious choices about eating and exercise, this practice will help you to know yourself as one possible way of being beautiful—all the time.

The relationship you have with your own body directly affects the quality and depth of all your relationships, especially intimate ones. As you learn to treat yourself with greater compassion and appreciation and to recognize your own beauty, you'll find it easier to connect with another human being on a profoundly intimate level.

3

Reducing Your Baggage

To make space in your life for a new relationship or to improve
your current one, it's time to start releasing anything you've
been holding on to that's preventing you from experiencing true
intimacy. This process will bring you to a level of self-awareness
that will give you more energy, insight, flexibility, and freedom,
making you much more available for the soulmate experience.

We often hear that someone has "too much baggage" to be ready for a committed, connected relationship. At forty, Kiran had been married and divorced twice. He still owns and operates a business with his first wife and a rental property with his second. When he started dating again after his second divorce, Kiran got the message time and time again that all this "baggage" was a big strike against him.

After three years of this sort of rejection, Kiran met Leah. Rather than seeing Kiran's former spouses as a burden, Leah saw them as an opportunity to get to know him better. "I would love to have met Kiran earlier in life, so it's great to have them around," she says.

"They tell me stories about him that go back to high school." Leah and Kiran have now been married for several years. "I'm very close to both his exes," she says. "I actually call them my sisters-in-law!" Now, who had the baggage here: Kiran, or the women he'd dated before meeting Leah?

Your relationship will eventually charge you for every ounce of baggage you check in with.

From Kiran's story, we can see that baggage isn't always what we think it is. It isn't necessarily our circumstances, our past, or even the issues we're currently working with. *Baggage is often just a lack of flexibility about accepting whatever is showing up in our life or someone else's.*

In the next few pages, you'll have the opportunity to conduct a thorough investigation of your own baggage—meaning anything that has the potential to keep you from truly connecting with another person. For this investigation to be most useful to you, don't skim through the material to find the "answers." Instead, commit to getting to know yourself better by fully exploring the ideas in this chapter. Be honest with yourself. At the same time, treat yourself with compassion: We *all* have baggage. What's important is recognizing our baggage and minimizing its effects on our relationships.

THE INSUFFICIENCY CONVERSATION

An underlying or recurring feeling of emptiness, loneliness, or longing is something many, if not most, of us have experienced at one time or another. No matter how rich our lives may be—with a satisfying career, material wealth, and plenty of friends—we may still be carrying around a low-level feeling that something important is missing. These feelings of lack are fed by an endless stream of negative thoughts about our lives and ourselves. Michael Naumer called this ongoing inner dialogue our "insufficiency conversation."

We've created many ways of distracting ourselves from our internal sense of lack. We escape through entertainment, hobbies, or addictions; fill our social calendars with activities and commitments; or even manifest constant drama. But the number one place many of us turn to in order to address our insufficiency conversation is our relationships.

The trouble is, everything a significant other can offer us—acknowledgment, encouragement, approval, acceptance—will never be enough to end our insufficiency conversation. Once we realize that a partner is not going to be the one to make us happy or give us everything we think we need to be complete, we're likely to feel disappointed, discouraged, and maybe even resentful.

The way out of this trap is to make a commitment to "being the one" who will address your *own* insufficiency conversation. When you no longer need your partner's validation, then any encouragement, love, or guidance your partner does offer you will be their very best, given freely and from a place of love. When validation is no longer the

We often unknowingly drag a suitcase full of problems into a new relationship, drop them at our partner's feet, and say, "Fix these for me!"

47

primary reason you're in a relationship, you can explore, enjoy, and appreciate everything that relationship has to offer.

Deborah, a preschool teacher, has experience with this. "Only recently did I admit to myself the extent of my neediness and the energy it has taken to hide that neediness from others. I have known deep disappointment in relationships because I was trying to have someone take away the bottomless pit of longing. The realization that no one else could make that go away for me is transforming my relationships."

"INTO ME I SEE"

Intimacy is sometimes translated as "into me you see" or, occasionally, as "into me I see." Because our relationships with others are really an extension of our relationship with ourselves, "into me I see" is essential for "into me you see" to be possible.

People who are willing to genuinely see themselves and unconditionally accept what they see are capable of a higher level of relationship. The more we know and accept ourselves—from our fears and insecurities to our motivations and talents—the more open, honest, and receptive we will be with others.

Self-intimacy is liberating. As we really come to know who we are, we become empowered: We feel more comfortable, confident, and effective in the world. Opportunities open up for us, opportunities that become apparent when we're no longer distracted by the things we've been covering up or avoiding looking at. Our newfound clarity also puts us in a better position to make positive changes in our lives.

Despite all we have to gain from increased self-intimacy, many of us—motivated by fears of rejection, embarrassment, or criticism—have devised endless ways to keep from seeing ourselves clearly. We often avoid people and situations that might make us look at ourselves too deeply. We shy away from introspective or soul-searching books and films; we're more comfortable with small talk than deep conversations. We use entertainment and the Internet as an escape. We avoid being alone by accepting invitations to events that don't interest us or staying in relationships long after they've ceased to be a positive experience.

Think of any ways you avoid having time to yourself. Do you keep overly busy with work, projects, email, or social media? Do you plan activities to fill every available evening and weekend? Do you turn on music or the television whenever there's a stretch of silence in the house?

When you're comfortable *with yourself,* you're likely to be comfortable *sharing yourself.*

If this sounds like you, you may be trying to avoid the feelings of loneliness, insecurity, or anxiety that surface when you're alone. Although it may seem counterintuitive, the only path to freedom is to stop trying to go *around* these feelings and to go *through* them instead. These fears, many of which you may have been carrying around since childhood, will remain with you until you finally allow them to be experienced.

Rather than running from your feelings of anxiety, loneliness, or self-doubt by calling a friend, surfing the Web, or turning on the news, learn to allow yourself to experience them completely. In this practice, the intention is to *process and release these emotions by fully feeling their effects in your body without adding to them with more negative thoughts.*

At first you might strongly resist this practice. You may have been avoiding doing exactly this because you are afraid the feelings will be overwhelming. What you will find, however, is that allowing your accumulated fears and repressed feelings to finally express themselves will actually begin to dissolve them.

As soon as possible after uncomfortable feelings arise, find a quiet place where you can be alone. Close your eyes and focus all of your attention on what you are experiencing. Let any thoughts that come in just drift by, and keep your attention on any physical sensations you're having. The idea is to *really feel the effects of the emotions you've been repressing.*

As you allow these emotions, which have been trapped inside you, to express themselves, you may experience a great wave of fear or intense sadness. Stay with it. As long as you're not feeding those feelings with more negative thoughts, you will eventually begin to experience a deep sense of relief, calmness, and even gratitude or peace.

To take this practice one step further, don't wait until your insufficiency conversation starts up on its own. You can tune into your buried fears and emotions by intentionally spending time alone, without the distraction of a computer, phone, or even a book. Just be quiet, watching for any feelings that arise and allowing yourself to fully experience them.

Some people use meditation to get in touch with feelings they've been denying or repressing. Vicky found that meditation helped her to heal from the ending of her marriage. "In order to be ready for an 'alive' relationship," she says, "I had to come to life again myself. I had to get very honest with myself about the anger and fear I'd been trying to avoid before I could feel the passion that lived in me too. Meditation was my way into and through those feelings."

DROP THE MASK

Another impediment to experiencing intimacy—not only with other people, but also with ourselves—is our ego. We might conceal who we really are by hiding behind our accomplishments, possessions, titles, makeup, or clothing. We might build ourselves up by putting other people down, even if only in subtle ways.

While an inflated ego may temporarily succeed in covering up feelings of insecurity or insufficiency, it makes true intimacy unavailable to us. Think about what it's like when two egos come up against each other. Both people know they're right, and neither

True self-worth does not depend on what others think of you.

is truly open to understanding the other's perspective. On the other hand, real self-worth will make you more available for authentic, heart-to-heart connections that go far beyond what most people experience.

As you review these suggestions, remember that the idea is not to eliminate your ego, but simply to raise your awareness of it.

- Watch for any ways in which you try to disguise who you are. If you are separated, out of shape, and forty-nine years old, avoid checking the "single," "athletic," and "40–45" boxes on your dating profile.

- Think about whether you ever pretend to be someone you're not. When Lauren tells people she holds degrees in fine arts and business administration, she avoids mentioning that they're from a junior college in the hopes that people will assume they are bachelor's or master's degrees.

- In what ways do you try to hide your motives? Are you sometimes evasive, or do you obscure the truth? Robert will say he doesn't like the food served in particular restaurants, when in reality what he doesn't like is that they don't serve alcohol.

- How do you try to cover up your insecurities? Andrew, who is five foot five, says, "I tend to act arrogant to hide my self-consciousness about my height."

Keep in mind that none of these behaviors is necessarily negative; it depends on the situation and your intention. What is crucial is to be aware of your motivation when you're engaging in them.

If you think you rarely do any of these things, you may be surprised to find that in fact you do, even if only on occasion or in very subtle ways. Jared recently separated from his wife and had to move out. In talking to the owner of one apartment, Jared felt compelled to mention that he owned a substantial piece of property on the other end of town. "The guy was obviously willing to rent to me already, so I didn't have to prove my creditworthiness," Jared says. "It was purely to show him that I wasn't just any prospective renter, but materially successful too."

- Notice when you're saying or doing something to impress others. Sometimes we ask questions merely to give ourselves the opportunity to offer our own opinion or story. ("Is your baby walking yet? Oh? Well, *my* son walked at nine months.") Or we might say something solely to demonstrate our intelligence or expertise. Melody says that to receive acknowledgment from her significant other, "I verbally list all the things I did that day to show how valuable I am." Aimee admits, "When I'm not feeling recognized for having good ideas and being intelligent, I'm likely to blurt out something I've done, at an inappropriate moment, and end up feeling really stupid." We might use status symbols to show we have good taste or are well off. Shaun says he buys clothes just for the brand and always has the latest high-tech gadgets.

Of course, it's certainly possible to enjoy and appreciate designer clothes or a precision watch or car without trying to boost your sense of self-worth through them. The idea is to be aware of your *motivation*.

- Watch for the tendency to do or say things solely for recognition.
- Be on the lookout for other signs of the ego in operation, such as monopolizing conversations or vying to be the center of attention. The need to be right is one of the most prevalent and insidious ways our ego tries to feel in control.

- Notice even the smallest ways in which you criticize or find defects in others to make yourself look better. "In my family, we always tried to make someone else look stupid so that we'd feel superior," Kaitlyn confesses. "I've spent a lot of time trying to undo this habit, yet I still find myself saying things that subtly put other people down." If you tend to be critical toward other people, keep in mind that when you put others down, you severely limit their ability to contribute to your life in a positive way.

- Increase your awareness of any effects the comparisons you make have on your life and your relationships. When you compare yourself to someone else in any way—how much you've accomplished, how successful you are, what you do for a living, what kind of car you drive—you set up a contest that artificially inflates your self-worth if you win and deflates it if you lose. As Aimee says, "I have a terrible habit of comparing myself to others—and I *always* come up short!"

  > Learn to see yourself
  > as "different from"
  > rather than
  > as "better than"
  > or "less than."

- Identify situations that commonly trigger an ego reaction in you, and bring more awareness to them. Matthew recognizes that when he has to navigate through a complicated voice mail system, he becomes increasingly irritated. By the time he gets through to a real person, he says, "I'm ready to bite their head off!" For others, it may be standing in line or waiting in traffic that activates an "I'm too important for this" reaction.

As you grow more aware of your ego, its influence over you will gradually lessen. You will naturally become more authentic, and your capacity for intimacy will expand.

RELEASE ADDICTIONS
AND UNHEALTHY HABITS

We also use addictions—from compulsive time-fillers to substance abuse—in an attempt to escape our feelings of insufficiency. There are many definitions of addiction, including what might be considered "healthy addictions," like compulsive exercise. What is an addiction for one person might be harmless entertainment or pleasure for another. The Internet, for example, is a valuable resource for millions of people. But with its instant access to games, shopping, chat rooms, social networking sites, and pornography, it's a hotbed of addiction for many others.

Depending on the degree of control our addictions have over us, we're likely to miss opportunities for experiencing real connection in our relationships. Over time, addictions can erode any connection we do have.

The more energy you have tied up in addictions, the less energy you have available for your *life*.

To work with your addictions, you must first acknowledge having them.

- To get in touch with your addictions, make a list of any activity or substance that has control over you in some way, has produced unwanted consequences, or leaves you feeling anxious, stressed, guilty, or ashamed. Consider both classic addictions—to substances like caffeine, alcohol, marijuana, and food—as well as activities such as compulsive shopping, obsessively checking for messages, or constantly manifesting drama in your life.

- Now examine your life for any other unconscious or compulsive habits or behaviors, like biting your nails, interrupting others, procrastinating, or being chronically late.

- Finally, list any activities that you feel you overindulge in but can't seem to ease up on, such as surfing the Web, watching television, or doing crossword puzzles.

When Rachel took the time to do this inquiry, she realized that her primary addiction doesn't even show up on most lists of addictions. Yet it's one of the most common, especially in today's fast-paced world. "My daily routines leave me no time or motivation to pursue my bigger dreams," she says. "My addiction, I realize—and what keeps me from reaching the true success I envision for myself— is constantly needing to fill any available time."

Once you've identified an addiction, it's time to fully investigate the harm it's been causing. Contemplate all the ways in which this behavior is detrimental. How does it affect your health? Your relationships? Your plans, dreams, or career? When John finally gathered the courage to look at the consequences of his pornography addiction, he saw that it left him with little motivation to spend time with his wife or kids. It also caused him to neglect his responsibilities at work and put his children in danger of being exposed to inappropriate material.

Now, rather than seeing your addiction as something you *have* (as in, "I have an addiction to . . ."), see it as a *choice* you make in each moment. In this way, the addiction becomes a day-to-day, moment-to-moment decision of whether to engage in this particular activity or not.

Don't beat yourself up for what you chose today. You can always make a different choice tomorrow.

James tried to cut back on his television watching for months, with little success. But once he started to see his addiction as a choice he made each day, he found it easier to simply choose something different. "I thought I'd try an experiment: turn it off for a week and see what happened. That week made all the difference."

With desire and determination, you can often make significant progress on your own toward lessening any addiction's influence over you. There are also many resources available to assist you in releasing yourself from the grip of anything you're ready to move on from. If you have issues with drugs or alcohol, a counselor or support group will not only be invaluable for helping you address your addiction, but also give you tools that will be useful in all areas of your life, including your relationships.

Once you've identified and acknowledged any addictive or habitual behaviors that may be getting in the way of your soulmate experience, ask yourself this question: *What is the best way to work with this addiction or habit?* Is it time to talk it over with a supportive friend, or to get the assistance of a counselor or group that's focused on this issue? Or do you have sufficient motivation and willpower to address it on your own, with inspiration and guidance from books, websites, friends, or family?

EMBRACE YOUR UNIQUE GIFTS

We all have special talents and abilities. Some of us know how to write well or cook a great meal. We may have a gift with children, a green thumb, or artistic ability. Many of us, though, have a tendency to downplay our gifts. As children, we may have been discouraged from even talking about ourselves or our accomplishments in a positive way. "Don't brag. Don't be a showoff." We often minimize or disregard our special talents and let our gifts go undeveloped and unappreciated.

Developing a greater awareness of your gifts is not being arrogant, superficial, or egotistical. In fact, cultivating your special abilities is a way to give back to the world. When we hide our gifts to any extent, we can't fully develop them, enjoy them, or share them. Any way in which we resist, ignore, or simply don't see who

Not seeing how beautiful, capable, or talented you are can be a barrier to real connection in your relationships.

we are puts us at a disadvantage when it comes to forming close, connected relationships. When we can acknowledge and embrace our gifts, we're in a position to put them to their best possible use.

If you're having trouble seeing your own gifts, you might ask a close friend or two this question: *What do you feel are my most positive qualities?* Know that if your friend sees these qualities in you, they are there—so take notes!

Many people brush aside compliments with a quick thank-you and a self-deprecating remark. The highest response you can give to a compliment, though, is to acknowledge the truth in it and open yourself up to that truth. The next time someone gives you compliment, you might consider simply saying, "Thank you for seeing that in me."

FREE YOURSELF FROM RESENTMENT

Resentments may be the heaviest baggage we carry around. Ironically, they may also be the easiest to let go of once we understand their true nature. *Resentment is the pain we feel when we believe someone else should have done something other than what they did.*

Resentment is closely related to regret, guilt, shame, and embarrassment. These are all types of pain we feel when we believe we should have done something other than what we did.

Although you can't erase the experiences you've had, you can radically change how you interpret the memories of those experiences today. Releasing your resentment doesn't mean you're condoning anyone's actions. It's something you do for *yourself* to finally stop re-creating your suffering every time you contemplate this aspect of your past.

We need to become conscious of the meaning we assign to our experiences,

**Every time
we interpret
a past experience
the same way
we have before,
we produce the same
emotional response.**

59

especially because we often attach meaning that makes us feel bad or otherwise disempowered. *We assign meaning to what we see by the lens we choose to look through.* For example, some of us interpret reality through the lens "lack of love." If Ashley's boyfriend doesn't call her, she might evaluate his behavior through this lens and decide the lack of a phone call means he doesn't care about her. Viewed through "lack of love," almost anything a significant other does—like not checking with us before making a decision, or forgetting to tell us about an old friend they heard from—can be seen as proof they don't love us. We believe in lack of love, so we see evidence of lack of love all around us.

If we interpret *anyone's* actions through the "lack of love" lens (or the "rejection" lens, or the "abandonment" lens, among countless others), we're bound to suffer in some way. What we need to do is interrupt our typical reaction and become aware of the lenses through which we're interpreting our experiences.

> We can free ourselves from the past by changing how we relate to it in the present.

Looking at your resentments and regrets through a new lens allows you to change the meaning you've assigned to the people and events in your life. When you choose to look through a new lens, you will transform your experience of those people or situations.

To begin the process of purging your resentments, sit down and make a list of any ways in which you blame other people (such as parents, siblings, friends, or previous lovers) for the circumstances or conditions of your life. Also make a note of any regrets you have about your past.

When you've got a list together, prioritize the items according to which resentments you think will be the easiest to let go of. Then experiment with the lenses described below. See how many of your resentments you can dissolve using one or another of these lenses.

The "This Isn't About My Value" Lens

If we have issues with our own value, we will often interpret what others do as meaning something about our value. The "this isn't about my value" lens will relieve much of the suffering caused by our beliefs that someone else's actions mean something about us.

Imagine that someone shows up a half hour late for your first date. You might decide that your date's tardiness means something about *you*. Charged up with all the evidence of how you've been slighted, you'll probably be noticeably irritable and dismissive by the time they actually arrive.

Suppose, though, that when you notice you're starting to get irritated, you make a choice to view the situation through the "this isn't about my value" lens. You could then easily decide to enjoy your time, even though your date is late (or may not show at all), by just appreciating being where you are: the view, the drink you ordered, the people watching. You might chat with the people at the next table or use the opportunity to craft a letter you've been meaning to write.

> We respect people who accept what we do and say without making it "mean" something.

When your date does show up, you might even be willing to take a risk and authentically share with him or her all that you'd been thinking about while you were waiting. Who knows? A real conversation like this could be the foundation for a fantastic relationship.

Many of us could benefit by having the "this isn't about my value" lens with us all the time. When our partner forgets to run an errand or doesn't pick up after themselves, we could take this as a reflection of how they feel about us and choose to feel resentful. Our experience will be much better, though, if we retrain ourselves not to interpret such actions as meaning our partner doesn't care about us.

The "Everyone Is Doing the Best They Can" Lens

When we're standing in judgment of someone, we may believe we could never have done what they did. But if you had lived that person's life, and had exactly that person's experiences and beliefs, it's very possible you would have done exactly the same thing.

Whenever you're in complaint about what someone else did or is doing, there's something about the situation that you don't know. If you knew the whole story—if you saw the situation clearly from all sides and from the perspectives of everyone involved—you might conclude that this person is doing the best they can, given their history, belief systems, experiences, and present circumstances.

Some people, for example, resent their parents for how they were raised. The "everyone is doing the best they can" lens enables us to see that even if our parents

> If you're in judgment of another person, you can be sure there's something about the situation you don't know.

were neglectful or abusive, it may very well have been the best they could do at the time. This change in perspective can greatly accelerate our healing process and give us the freedom to move on.

Alyssa had been raised single-handedly by her father, an abusive alcoholic. She used the "everyone is doing the best they can" lens to look back at her childhood and all the things she resented about the way her father had treated her.

"At first I wanted to keep arguing that there was no excuse for what he'd done to me," she said, "but then it occurred to me that he'd had no good role models: His father had abused him, and probably *his* father before that. He had no concept of how to raise a daughter, especially on his own. He was in way over his head. I could

> You can't change
> the experiences
> you had,
> but you can change
> your experience
> of them today.

see that, given his background, I could have been just as poor a parent as he was." Alyssa now feels at peace with her past. "What my father did was wrong in the sense that it was no way to treat a child, or any human being. He's still not someone I'd choose to spend time with. But I realized that the anger I'd carried around for so long was really *self*-abuse. I'm so glad to be free of it."

This lens is also powerful when you apply it to yourself. When turned inwards, it becomes the "I'm doing the best I can" lens.

Suppose that for years you've been burdened with guilt from an abortion you had as a teenager. If you'd known then what you know now, you might have chosen differently. But you didn't. Carrying this guilt is of no use to you. And if you should ever want to use your experience to help others—by counseling someone in a similar situation, for instance—you'll be much more effective coming from a place of understanding rather than from a place of guilt.

The "People Are Miraculous Surprises" Lens*

Although it may seem odd at first, the "people are miraculous surprises" lens can come in handy when we find ourselves in judgment of others.

Zena and Ethan divorced after being married for fifteen years and parenting two children together. "For the first couple of years afterward," Zena says, "I resented that he'd left me for someone else, without any warning or time for me to adjust. And I resented him because he was happy and I wasn't." Eventually Zena came to the realization that she didn't have to keep suffering. She could instead choose to see Ethan through the lens "people are miraculous surprises" and just appreciate him for what he *does* contribute to her life.

Resentments about our previous partner, if we don't heal and release them, often lead to expectations about our next one.

"He's still a great father to our kids. He provides for them. He even helps me out when I need a hand with projects around the house, even though he no longer lives here." Zena says that interacting with Ethan (which she's going to be doing the rest of her life) is more pleasant when she sees him through this lens.

---

* This and the next lens owe their origins to Michael Naumer.

Staci tells of a close friend who was going through a difficult period and moved in with her for a few months while she got her life together. "One morning, I came into my kitchen and spotted a pool of water on the floor under the water dispenser. My friend had apparently gotten a drink in the night and left the valve on the dispenser open. My lovely bamboo floor was now permanently rippled where the water had sat on it overnight. When I felt the resentment rising, I remembered the 'people are miraculous surprises' lens. In that moment, I saw that I could use this imperfection in my floor as a reminder of how precious friendships are. That daily reminder to cherish my friendships is a gift given to me by this wonderful woman."

> You'll stop forming new resentments when you learn to use these lenses the moment something triggers a reaction in you.

The "Just One Possible Way of Being Human" Lens

If you're not quite ready to see someone as a miraculous surprise, try the "just one possible way of being human" lens. It often works when the other lenses don't. We could call it the lens of last resort.

"I find it useful when I simply can't believe someone is doing what they're doing," Brett says. "It helps put things into perspective."

The "just one possible way of being human" lens can help us gently let go of our prejudices. Keene had always been uncomfortable when people asked him for spare change. He would avoid making eye contact with them and brush them off with a mumbled "No, no, I don't" and a dismissive wave of his hand. Now he says, "When someone asks me for money these days, I think, 'This person is just one possible way of being human,' and any judgment I have immediately dissipates. I'm then in a better position to decide what kind of response I'd like to make to this particular person. At the very least, I look them in the eye and smile, and feel good about that."

WHAT IF MY PARTNER ISN'T INTERESTED IN REDUCING *THEIR* BAGGAGE?

Some people who are actively reducing their own baggage may find themselves with a partner who isn't interested in doing the same. Baggage, you may remember, is anything that has the potential to keep you from a truly connected relationship. If your partner has an issue that significantly affects the quality of your relationship—such as jealousy, anger, or a serious addiction they haven't addressed—it's easy to feel confused and overwhelmed.

You have three choices when your partner isn't interested in taking responsibility for their own behavior.

Your first choice is to continue responding to the situation as you have been, whether that's trying to help your partner recognize or address their issue, or getting angry, or withdrawing. We may make this choice for years before we come to the understanding that, for now, our partner simply isn't ready to change. Until your partner asks for your help in some way, pressuring him or her to change will only result in frustration and resentment for both of you.

Your second choice is to leave. This can be a very difficult decision to make, especially if there are children involved or you have been together a long time. Many people don't make this choice until they've spent years struggling to improve their relationship. It's almost always the best choice for someone who's in an abusive or violent situation. If you're in such a situation, know that there are support groups, services, and shelters available to you. There really *are* people with open and loving hearts who are ready to help.

If you make this second choice—to leave—do your best to do so from a place of love and compassion, with both you and your partner's best interests in mind. Whether or not your partner is able to come from a place of love as well, the transition will be smoother for both of you even if only you can (and even if only some of the time). You'll also accumulate much less baggage this way, making it easier for you to be receptive to and ready for a new relationship when that time comes.

Your third choice—and often the most transformative—is to stay for the time being but to *change your experience*. You do this by acknowledging that you're choosing to remain in the relationship for now and that your partner's behavior is a given for the time being. In essence, you do your best to accept the conditions in which you find yourself—*for now*.

> Every relationship
> we have
> offers us
> the perfect
> opportunities
> to grow
> and expand.

Making the choice to change your experience will free up the energy you've been spending in resistance and allow you to put more energy and focus into all the things you *do* love about your life. It will give you space to *breathe*.

By becoming more aware of anything that might be preventing you
from being open and authentic, you will create a healthy
inner environment for being in relationship. Reducing your baggage—
whether taking responsibility for your insufficiency conversation,
bringing awareness to your ego and your addictions,
learning to embrace and develop your gifts,
or freeing yourself from resentment—
makes you much more available for the soulmate experience.

4

Raising Your Soulmate Potential

*Millions of us dream of experiencing a deeply connected relationship
that grows richer and more intimate with time. We believe that
our soulmates—with whom we're emotionally, physically, and
. spiritually in sync—are out there somewhere, if only we knew how
to find them. For most of us, though, a soulmate relationship won't
suddenly appear when, by some stroke of cosmic luck, we stumble
across the one person on the planet who's perfectly compatible with us.
Rather than leaving it to fate, there are changes you can make right
now that will invite the soulmate experience into your life.*

Almost daily, we're inundated with the message that if we buy the
right product, do the right exercises, wear the right clothes, or
search in the right place, we will find "the one." But let's be realistic.
If these approaches to finding our ideal companion really worked,
the divorce rate would plummet and more people would be enjoying
healthier, happier relationships.

The problem is, just going out and searching for "the one" is not enough. Online dating sites offer us "highly compatible matches" based on details about our personalities, values, interests, and goals. But the truth is that even a seemingly ideal match will begin to lose its luster over time if both people aren't developing and nurturing qualities that will continually breathe new life into their relationship.

So the first question to ask is not "How can I *find* my soulmate?" but "How can I *be* a soulmate?"

Being a soulmate is an approach to life. You don't need to have resolved all of your issues or have sky-high self-esteem to attract the enlightened relationship you desire. What *is* required, though, are these two things:

- First, you need a willingness to take responsibility for your own experience in your relationships. If you've been using even some of the ideas in Chapters 1, 2, and 3, you already have this.

- Second, you need a desire to cultivate qualities that will make all your relationships more playful, meaningful, and alive— qualities like those described in this chapter.

With these two things, not only will you become more available for a soulmate relationship; you will also be able to more easily identify others who are available for one. More precisely, you'll be in a position to *create* your soulmate experience. And you may find that a lot easier— and more rewarding—than just waiting for one to "land" on you!

APPROACHING LIFE
IN A SPIRIT OF DISCOVERY

Rather than allowing life to simply happen to them, people with a high degree of "soulmate potential" view their lives as ongoing opportunities for exploration and self-discovery. They're always on the lookout to see where their beliefs, attitudes, and habits are holding them back or aren't producing the experiences they'd like. They're open to trying new things, even knowing they might feel uncomfortable in the process. They're also open to seeing the world through other people's eyes and are willing to shift their own perspective whenever they see an opportunity for growth or connection.

What we avoid seeing in ourselves will affect us in ways we can't imagine. "Whatever you have that you don't want others to see—*that's* the stuff that gets between you and your relating," Michael Naumer would say. Uncovering and acknowledging self-defeating behaviors—or recognizing when we're being manipulative, blaming, or judgmental, for example—can be scary, and even embarrassing, but people with soulmate potential are up to the challenge. Rather than disguising or burying their fears, they make an effort to draw them out so they can explore and understand them. Instead of ignoring or hiding from the unresolved issues of their past, they continue to search for ways to uncover and heal them.

People who approach life in a spirit of discovery know that every experience and interaction can help them in their pursuit to see themselves more clearly. When challenges arise, rather than backing away, they welcome the insights that come through investigating them. They use everything that shows up to see themselves better. For instance, when they observe themselves complaining, they might notice a lack of gratitude for all they *do* have. If they habitually arrive late, they may see their own lack of organization, tendency to overcommit, or arrogance. If they find themselves being rude to someone, they might see their own sense of entitlement or self-importance. They know that just noticing these behaviors will naturally shift them into more effective and loving ways of relating.

These people seek to go below the surface and truly connect with others. They're less interested in what degrees you've earned, how much money you make, or what kind of car you drive than they are in exploring and appreciating the more meaningful aspects of life with you.

One useful tool for helping you approach life in this spirit of discovery is the question *What is there for me to learn here?* Whenever you feel resistance in yourself to anything—ideas, situations, events, or people—this question will help you break through that resistance and find ways to make the most of what you're experiencing.

When someone expresses an opinion that's different from yours, ask yourself, *What is there for me to learn here?* This will greatly reduce the need to justify your position or defend yourself in some way. Instead, you're likely to find yourself authentically connecting with this person

> **What is there for me to learn here?** can shift your focus from "what's wrong" to "what's possible."

and genuinely interested in understanding their perspective. *What is there for me to learn here?* can be revealing whenever you're resisting what is going on right now—whether that takes the form of boredom during a graduation ceremony, impatience as you visit with your partner's relatives, or frustration at your intermittent computer troubles.

BEING OPEN TO
WHATEVER SHOWS UP

People with a high degree of soulmate potential know that letting go of unnecessary judgments and expectations about the world and what happens in it will help them flow through life with a minimum of effort. They rarely have strongly held positions about how things should be. This doesn't mean they adopt an artificially positive attitude or deny what's happening or what they're feeling. It means they continually grow in their ability to accept "what is," *including* what's happening and what they're feeling.

These people also apply this attitude to their relationships. Rather than having numerous expectations about what other people should or shouldn't do, they seek to approach everyone with openness and receptivity. When it comes to our primary relationships, this one shift in attitude can mean the difference between a miserable experience and an extraordinary one.

> Knowing how to find something positive in the most negative-looking circumstances is the greatest secret of truly happy people.

So how do we make that shift? First, we need to understand that we have two choices about how to respond to anything in our lives. We can respond from a place of resistance, or we can respond from a place of acceptance. We all know what we get when we resist: instant feelings of irritation, frustration, or anger. We might hear ourselves saying things like "I won't be comfortable if Jerome brings his new girlfriend to the party" or "I can't concentrate with fluorescent lighting. I'm not going to get much out of this conference." Attitudes like these have an enormous effect on how our experiences unfold. When we can accept what's happening *as it happens*, we feel like we're flowing *with* life rather than against it.

Accepting "what is" right now doesn't mean we condone a situation or give up our ability to improve it. In fact, if we aren't wasting our energy in resistance, we'll have more energy for adjusting to our ever-changing circumstances.

Suppose your flight was delayed for hours and you arrive at your destination much later than anticipated. At the rental counter, you discover that the car you'd reserved has been given to someone else and there are none left. You snap at the agent, raising your voice so that she (and everyone else) knows how upset you are. While you're busy insisting that something be done and demanding to see a manager, another passenger, who's also been denied a car, decides to try the agency a few yards away. You're still arguing with the agent, who simply has nothing to offer you, as your fellow passenger drives off in the last available car.

When you accept what's happening rather than resist it, you can shift your focus to identifying and pursuing other possibilities.

74

Even mild opposition to a situation prevents us from getting all we can from it, so we need to learn to recognize the signs that we're going into resistance. That observation alone will interrupt our habitual negative response. It's often easier to catch ourselves just before we begin to resist than when we're in the midst of a reaction. That's because as we justify and defend our position, our resistance increases, making it even harder for us to "wake up" to what we're doing.

> **The more aware you are, the less often you will get hooked into a negative reaction.**

Being open to whatever shows up means understanding that the one thing we can depend on is that everything changes. *True strength comes from how much flexibility we have to adapt to our constantly changing world.*

DISCOVERING THE HIDDEN GIFTS

People with well-developed soulmate potential know that even the most challenging circumstances, situations, or people have something of value to offer. This isn't being naive or unrealistic. It's the simple recognition that things won't always go our way. Schedules change, cars and computers eventually need repair, and at some point we're going to encounter long lines, rudeness, and rush-hour traffic. These people know that their experience of these events is directly linked to how they approach them.

One of the easiest ways to discover the gift in a challenging situation or encounter is to ask yourself, *What's the best use I can make of this experience? What opportunity might this experience be bringing me?* These questions can help you see possibilities when you couldn't before.

If you're dealing with an irritable, antagonistic coworker, you might see this as an opportunity to learn more effective communication techniques for handling such situations. If your relationship has recently ended, you might recognize this as the perfect time to pursue a dream you've had on hold, such as moving to a new city or getting more involved in a particular cause. Or if you encounter an overly aggressive salesperson, you could use the situation to practice staying grounded.

Searching for potentially positive aspects or outcomes in the midst of a difficult situation doesn't deny the seriousness of the circumstances or any pain or grief you and others might be experiencing. On the contrary—focusing on the positive may well give you (and everyone involved) encouragement, confidence, and strength. Qualities like these are very beneficial in the face of challenging circumstances.

> Remember to look for the hidden gifts when you catch yourself in complaint—whether about your job, your neighbors, your family, or the weather.

Erin and her daughter Karlyn were leaving soon for orientation week at Karlyn's new college. Four days before their trip, Erin's ex-husband called to say that he was coming too. Erin was fuming.

"It's just like Bill to do this to me at the last minute. I've been looking forward to spending time with Karlyn before she's off on her own forever. Bill had no interest in going three months ago. Now he wants to share our hotel room!"

When Erin was asked whether there was anything positive that could come from this change in plans, she was adamant. "Absolutely not. Karlyn says it's fine if he comes, but *I'll* be miserable. This is going to be a horrible trip."

If Erin had been able to see that her resistance wouldn't benefit her in any way—she wasn't going to change Bill's mind, and Karlyn might be left with negative memories of her first days at college—she may have been able to look for a potential gift in this turn of events. Even finding the smallest positive aspect to focus on would have helped her to view the situation from a more optimistic perspective.

For example, Erin might have recognized that this could be a positive experience for their daughter: Karlyn might appreciate having both her parents with her as she takes such a large step toward independence. Karlyn might also come to see that divorce doesn't have to mean that two people can never be kind and loving toward each other again.

With this small shift, Erin might also realize that it's time to find ways to work through her lingering anger and sadness over the ending of her marriage. Although the marriage is over, her relationship with Bill will certainly continue into the foreseeable future. Acknowledging and releasing her feelings would give all three of them a better experience.

SEEKING A HIGHER POSSIBILITY

When faced with challenging circumstances, people with a high degree of soulmate potential strive to stay open to other ideas, options, and approaches. They've learned that there is another possibility in any situation, even if it's not obvious at first.

Jeanne, a spunky seventy-something, lives in a townhouse. The woman next door has a grandson who likes to hang out on the patio while listening to rap music and smoking. The sounds and smoke drift right into Jeanne's windows, which she prefers to keep open. Jeanne had asked the young man several times to turn the volume down, but soon the music would be going full blast again. She also bought him a smokeless ashtray, but he didn't seem inclined to use it.

Jeanne was frustrated with the situation for months, until she finally got fed up with keeping her windows closed and feeling like a prisoner in her own home. So she sat down and asked herself, *What's possible here?*

Jeanne realized that although she prefers not to smell cigarette smoke, she feels that, at her age, she really doesn't need to worry about cancer. A higher possibility for her, she decided, was to let the smoke and noise be reminders to be grateful that her senses were still sharp. This shift in perspective

When you're faced with a dilemma or when something isn't going your way, ask yourself, *What's possible here?*

brought her an immediate feeling of peace. One day she even found herself standing up and beginning to move to the music she found so offensive—getting some welcome exercise in the process.

This solution may not work for everyone, but it worked for Jeanne. If she had stayed stuck in her position, she says, she would have continued to resist the young man's behavior and done nothing except add to her own frustration. She certainly wouldn't be getting up to dance! What Jeanne had learned was this: *Once we've taken all reasonable steps to alleviate a difficult situation, what's left is to find a higher possibility.*

Approaching life in a spirit of discovery, being open to whatever shows up,
looking for the hidden gifts, seeking a higher possibility:
These are all moment-to-moment choices you can make
about how to approach the world and your relationships.
By making these choices more often, you will increase
your potential for experiencing connections that grow richer
and more intimate over time. You'll also find it much easier
to recognize someone else with soulmate potential.

Part 2

Keeping Your Soulmate Experience Alive

Every bit as important
as attracting your soulmate
is continually creating an environment for
your soulmate experience to blossom.
Such an environment encourages
ever-deepening intimacy
and allows you both to discover
joy, love, and satisfaction
in all aspects of your lives together.

5

Having a Guest in Your Life

The ways in which you approach your significant other will
greatly influence the kinds of experiences you have together.
Learning to treat your partner as an honored guest in your life will
go a long way toward creating the rich, fulfilling relationship you
imagine for yourself. In addition to keeping your connection fresh
and alive, treating your partner as a guest in your life will bring
a feeling of harmony and happiness to your everyday experiences.

At the start of a relationship, everything is new and exciting. We can't wait to get together with this person and learn everything we can about them. So many possibilities seem to be opening up for us, and our life feels passionate and full. People can tell just by looking at us that something special is going on: "Let me guess—you're in love!"

If we're like most people, we are also on a high because our new relationship is giving us all the validation we think we could ever want—but sooner or later, we're going to come tumbling down from that relationship high. No one out there can ever give us enough validation or make us feel special enough. No matter how loving, caring, or devoted our new partner is, he or she will never be the solution for our insufficiency conversation.

Because this basis for relationship is inherently unstable, we then try to stabilize it with rules and agreements. These rules may be explicit, informal, or unspoken. We think that if we make the right agreements in the beginning, we'll be able to capture the experience we're having now and preserve it for the future.

In addition to any rules or guidelines that couples might establish, most people come to a relationship with distinct sets of assumptions. These assumptions are often unexamined and unexpressed. But *agreements and assumptions won't produce the kind of relationship we want.* Instead of preserving or prolonging the excitement and life in a vibrant relationship, agreements and assumptions soon fill it with expectations. These expectations can be so destructive to a relationship that an entire chapter of this book is devoted to them (see Chapter 8).

It's no surprise that we approach our relationships in this fashion. The vast majority of us have grown up without the benefit of an intentional "relationship education." Think about it. Where did you get *your* relationship training? From watching your parents and others interacting? From television, books, or movies? If you're like most people, the relationship education you received was inadequate for preparing you to have extraordinary relationships. Relationship is one of the most important aspects of our lives, and many of us are struggling to get by with the only model available to us—a model that falls far short of creating the relationships we know are possible.

THE CONVENTIONAL MODEL FOR RELATIONSHIP

The majority of relationships we see around us are generally based on one model. Though all of the characteristics below might not apply to your relationships, chances are you've at least witnessed each of them at one time or another. The conventional model for relationship produces characteristics like these:

- We view our partner as someone to complete us or to make us feel whole.

- We shield our partner from new possibilities because we're afraid that if they know what they're missing out on, they won't want to be with us.

- We stop fully listening to our partner because we feel we've heard it all before.

- We assign blame to our partner when we feel they're not meeting our needs.

- We become embarrassed or angry when our partner does something that we feel reflects poorly on us.

- We use manipulation, guilt, anger, and withdrawal to try to ensure that our partner consistently meets our expectations.

- If our partner steps out of the routine that's been established, we see it as a threat to the relationship.

- Complaint becomes a normal part of our everyday conversations.

- We react with jealousy when our partner shows interest in other people.

- As time goes on, we begin to treat our partner more like a housemate and less like a lover.

- After a while, we become quicker to judge, criticize, and blame, and less likely to give our partner the benefit of the doubt.

All of these behaviors lead to our partner slowly closing off parts of themselves to us. Not knowing how to stop this process, we become resigned to the idea that this is just what eventually happens in a relationship.

You can see that the conventional model for relationship is based, for the most part, on fear. Afraid of losing what we have, we try to protect and contain our relationship to keep it from changing. In the process, we inadvertently squeeze the life out of it, and our relationship begins to feel more like a burden than a blessing.

Back when people had to struggle to survive and their primary focus was on acquiring adequate food and shelter, this model served an important function by helping to keep families together. Even today, a traditional relationship, particularly when the roles are well defined, can

> **You can't simultaneously control someone and have a soulmate experience with them.**

work on certain levels. But for many of us, the conventional model is dull and unfulfilling. It also won't produce the enlightened, soulmate experiences that we're longing for and know are possible.

THE SOULMATE MODEL
FOR RELATIONSHIP

While the conventional model for relationship is based primarily on fear, the soulmate model is based on something entirely different: freedom. Though many people find this idea unnerving, when we give ourselves and our partner freedom, our relationship continues to feel alive and compelling. What does a relationship under the soulmate model look like?

- We commit to taking responsibility for ourselves, including our beliefs, our attitudes, our issues, and our decisions.

- We see our partner as someone to enhance us rather than as someone to complete us.

- We know that being in relationship together is an ongoing choice.

- We support our partner's growth and evolution, even when it's scary.

- We use our individual and shared experiences as opportunities to keep our connection alive.

- We strive to see our partner and ourselves as clearly as possible and to accept who and where we each are right now.

- We watch for and do our best to minimize expectations and judgments.

- We understand that it's natural for us both to be attracted to other people.

- We're grateful for every day that this incredible human being chooses to be in our life.

Imagine what it would feel like to be in a relationship like this. Instead of becoming stale or dragging us down, our relationship continues to be a source of inspiration, excitement, and true connection. Without the pressures and struggles of the conventional model, our relationship can take place in a more harmonious and joyful state.

SHIFTING FROM A CONVENTIONAL RELATIONSHIP TO A SOULMATE RELATIONSHIP

Making the shift from a conventional relationship to a more enlightened way of relating involves changing how you approach your relationships. One sure way to start that shift is to begin to treat your partner as a guest in your life. We're not talking about the kind of guest who's an imposition: expecting you to entertain them, overstaying their welcome, and leaving a mess behind. That sort of guest requires considerable time and energy. We're talking about the kind of guest you love to be with—someone who enhances your life rather than weighs it down.

When you have a guest like this, you feel honored that they would appear in your life and hang out for a while. You offer them a safe, loving space from which they can discover new things about themselves and the world. You allow them the freedom to come and go as they please. You know your time with them is limited, so you make the most of it. Rather than wasting it in complaint or other negativity, you look for every opportunity to experience and share all the joys of life with them.

> **The soulmate model encourages and sustains the aliveness that is present at the start of a relationship.**
>
>

Treating your significant other as a guest in your life means all of the above. It means remembering that they are with you out of their own free will. It means knowing that they are capable of following their own path and making their own decisions. It means having gratitude for whatever time you get to spend together.

Breaking the Orbit

Have you ever noticed that people in conventional relationships often start to orbit around each other? You can see this in couples who need to check with each other before making even the most inconsequential decisions, or in people who are uncomfortable or insecure doing anything without their partner by their side.

Tatiana learned about the detrimental effects of orbiting the summer she was twenty. "I left behind a relationship that had grown stale and spent two and a half months traveling on my own. It was hard to return to school that fall after a summer-long adventure, but the first day back I met a handsome, intelligent guy and we began dating.

It was about three weeks later, when I was walking to class, that I realized I was having thoughts like 'What's he doing right now? What about the girls in his classes? Is he attracted to them?' I was stunned. After ten weeks of being independent and free, I found myself feeling anxious and unsure!"

> We never improve our relationships by obsessing about our partner.

Tatiana had discovered a simple but profound truth about relationships: *The moment we immerse ourselves in fearful thoughts about what our lover is thinking, or indulge in speculation about their motives or intentions, we disconnect from ourselves and instantly feel uncertain and insecure.* We feel much more grounded and secure when we focus internally, on our *own* experience, than when we focus externally, caught up in our ideas about someone *else's* experience.

When we have a guest, we allow them the freedom to make their own choices and to come and go as they please. In the beginning stages of a relationship, we do the same for our partner. We enter into a relationship as independent, sovereign human beings, but then—very soon, for some people—something starts to shift. Once we begin to develop a new identity for ourselves as one half of a couple, we may start to feel threatened by our partner's independence and try to rein them in. As we exchange more of our individual identity for this half-of-a-couple identity, we may feel incomplete and insecure when our partner is off being independent without us.

Typically, we use subtle methods of control at first: "I know you've taken ski trips by yourself for years, but if you decide to go next weekend, I'll probably be depressed the whole time." Later on, we become more direct: "Going skiing by yourself is called being single— and you're not single any more!"

Michael Naumer would advise us to "break the orbit and stay related." The more freedom our partner has to continue discovering themselves, the more they will enjoy (and appreciate) being with us. If you hold onto someone too tightly, you have a prisoner. If you offer someone a loving space to develop and grow, you have a lover. Although this may feel scary, in truth it's an indicator that your relationship is fully alive.

> Our partner's freedom is not something we grant— it's something we honor.

Your Partner Doesn't Owe You Anything

The conventional model for relationship comes with certain requirements, especially once we decide to make our relationship exclusive. There's an unspoken agreement that because you're now in a relationship, your partner "owes" you things—such as respect, love, or understanding. Not only that, but they're supposed to know exactly how and when you want or need these things. Of course, respect, love, and understanding are some of the primary reasons we're in a relationship. But to be authentic and truly satisfying, these things must be given freely, not insisted upon or coerced.

We think that meeting our needs is our partner's *responsibility*. We often expect this one person to meet a wide assortment of needs: physical, psychological, financial, social, sexual, spiritual. But need fulfillment isn't a healthy foundation for a relationship. In addition, as Michael Naumer pointed out, "If your partner meets all your needs and they leave, what do you lose? Everything you need!"

This may be hard for some people to swallow, but it's not our partner's job to meet our needs. In fact, *the healthiest way to be in a relationship is to take responsibility for your own needs.*

When we believe it's our significant other's obligation to attend our family reunions or company picnics by virtue of being our partner, we may find ourselves with a reluctant date rather than an enthusiastic one. As Sebastian said about his former marriage, "The more guilt she laid on me to do things with her, the more I resisted—and the less I enjoyed myself if I did end up going." Our partner will be much more likely to want to accompany us when they feel

> The more
> we think we need
> from our
> relationship,
> the less joy
> it can bring us.

their presence isn't just the fulfillment of an expectation. To create an environment that encourages your partner's willing participation, you might practice using invitation rather than expectation (see Chapter 8).

People who treat their significant other as a guest in their life respect their partner's free will. They endeavor to always give their partner the freedom to choose. They do their best never to use guilt or coercion to influence their partner's decisions. Their partner is free to join them on any particular adventure because they *choose* to, not because they feel they *should*.

When you begin to feel blame or resentment toward your partner, you might remind yourself, "My partner doesn't owe me anything."

You'll feel the grip of your resentment begin to relax. This will create space for you to approach your partner in a more receptive way. Don't be surprised if he or she suddenly seems different to you!

Your Partner's Actions Don't Mean Anything About Your Value

When we first start dating someone, it's natural to treat them as we would a guest. We're open to who they are and how they express themselves. Then, after we've been together awhile, we may slowly begin to discourage them from engaging in certain behaviors or activities. As a result, the person who was at ease interacting with other people becomes guarded and cautious about where they look and in whom they show interest. Before you know it, it's not nearly as enjoyable to spend an evening out together.

This deterioration is, in part, a product of the belief that what our partner does or doesn't do means something about our own value. For example, you may believe that if your partner chats with someone else while you're out to dinner together, or chooses to spend an evening with friends rather than with you, it means he or she cares more about someone else than about you.

Or suppose your partner forgets your birthday. You might interpret their forgetfulness as a sign they don't care, although the reality might be far different. Your partner may have been distracted by work, tired from lack of sleep, or just bad at remembering dates. Whatever the reason, the fact that he or she forgot doesn't mean anything about your value—as a partner *or* as a person.

We may also believe that our partner's actions (at least those we don't approve of) reflect poorly on us. Julia often feels embarrassed by her husband in public: "He tells dumb jokes and then laughs at them when no one else does. I can't stand it." Julia's underlying belief is that if she's married to someone who tells dumb jokes, it means *she's* dumb too.

One reason
people avoid
long-term relationships
is they know they'll
be expected
to give up
certain aspects
of who they are.

Elaine and Jordan have been living together for two years. In the last few months, Elaine has become frustrated with the fact that Jordan doesn't seem to have as much interest in sex as she does. "He's always telling me how beautiful and sexy I am, but he rarely comes on to me. I pretty much have to start things up every time," Elaine says. "Once we get started, everything's fine—but I want *him* to get things going. I've even counted to see how long it'd be if I waited for him. You know how long? Three weeks!" Elaine finds herself feeling so angry and hurt that she can't even speak to Jordan about the topic.

When Elaine believes that Jordan's apparent lack of libido means something about her value, she shuts herself off from him. If she were able to stay open to Jordan and remember that whatever is going on for him, his actions (or non-actions) don't reflect on her worth as a person, the situation would be less difficult for her. She would also be in a much better place to think of new approaches to energize their sexual connection.

Be Aware of What You're Expressing

When we have visiting guests, we may be more aware of our attitudes and behaviors than we are with the people we see every day. We're less likely to be disagreeable or temperamental, or to create a lot of drama. With people we interact with every day, it's easier to fall into the habit of being indifferent or even negative on a regular basis.

Have you noticed that many people seem to live their lives in a state of low-grade complaint? They may greet their partner at the door with remarks like "I can't believe how bad the traffic was on the way home! And the office was freezing today. I'm exhausted and cold and now I have to make dinner, but there's nothing here I'm even in the mood for." Or they may continually talk about minor grievances in the hopes of getting others to agree with them so they'll feel justified in feeling the way they do. People often have entire conversations that are nothing more than a familiar exchange of gripes.

Take a week's vacation from complaint and notice the difference it makes in your life.

It's important to become aware of just how much our attitudes can and do affect the people around us. Although we may think such offhand complaining is harmless, putting out negative energy will often cause others to either join you in negativity or withdraw from you altogether. By growing more conscious of how we choose to express ourselves, we will increase our ability to have a connected experience with anyone we happen to be with.

Stay Open to Who Your Partner Is Right Now

There is a story of a brilliant scientist who developed a brain tumor that destroyed his ability to form short-term memories. After he became ill, his wife grew tired of having to answer the same questions from him over and over. Eventually she hired a companion to take care of him. The companion was taken by the man's interest in life and his stories of the world. Each time she visited, the man was delighted with her as well and would fall in love with her, as if for the first time. The woman did not mind his loss of memory. In fact, she appreciated it. Where else would she meet a brilliant man who would fall in love with her time and time again?

> In many relationships, the longer you know someone, the less you're able to really see them.

One reason relationships are so exciting at the beginning is that there's so much unknown. But after spending a significant amount of time together, we think we know who our partner is: their likes and dislikes, their motivations, their desires, even what they're experiencing in a given situation. All the unknown, we believe, is now known—and there goes the excitement.

What's really happened is that we've formed a set of fixed ideas about our partner and are now relating to them *through those ideas.* Your partner is constantly evolving, as are you. But your pictures from the past can greatly distort who you see in the present. Many couples spend years relating almost exclusively like this and are no longer able to truly see each other.

The deep sense of familiarity shared by two people who love each other is one of the most wonderful aspects of a close, long-term relationship. We get into trouble, though, when we begin to think we know everything about our partner.

> It's not our partner's responsibility to show up differently.
> It's our responsibility to see them differently.

Watch for any ideas or assumptions you form about who your partner is or what they should or shouldn't do. You might make a list of all the ideas and assumptions you have about them, everything you can think of. You may be surprised by how long your list is! Now consider how this collection of assumptions locks you into a particular idea about who your partner is.

When you are receptive to who your partner is in this moment, as you would be with a guest, the possibility opens for you to see something new in them instead of continuing to see the "same old" person. As Dylan, a graphic designer, says about his girlfriend, "It's important for me to always try to see Sara as someone new. It's something I do for *me*, not for her. I want to be in a relationship where I'm excited about who I'm with!"

When we find ourselves becoming irritated with something our significant other does, we can shift away from the blame we're feeling by taking responsibility for our own experience. For example, Kim was expressing frustration that her love life with her husband had become stale. Why does he always kiss me the same way, she would wonder.

Rather than putting the blame on her partner, Kim could choose to take responsibility for her reaction. Dropping her judgment and blame will create the space for her to experience his kiss differently, move the kiss in another direction, or even take the initiative to suggest that they have fun experimenting with different ways of kissing.

When you're listening to your loved one tell a story you've heard before, it may be that you simply relax and sink into that sweet, comfortable feeling of familiarity. But if you find yourself getting annoyed instead, take a moment to shift your focus. Remind yourself that neither of you is exactly the same person you were a week ago, much less a year ago, or ten. If you listen without preconceptions, you're bound to hear something new and maybe even gain some unexpected insight.

"Lyle always likes to tell the story of how we met," Rose says. "Each time I hear it, I try to listen as though it's the first time and I don't know him. I experience it a little differently every time."

Even if we've been used to taking someone for granted, which is easy to do if we're not paying attention, we really can learn to start seeing them in new ways. Ask Amy, whose marriage of over twenty years seemed to be crumbling around her—until she and her husband decided to try a new approach to their relationship. "Enjoying who each of us is *right now* saved our marriage," she says.

Put Your Trust in Something Trustworthy

When people are asked to name the most important factors in creating a successful relationship, trust usually appears near the top of the list. What many of us think of as trust, though, really isn't trust at all.

Think about this. We may claim to trust our partner, but then when they do something we don't want them to do, we say they've "violated our trust" and we take our trust away from them. This kind of trust is really just control in disguise. By having this type of "trust" for our partner—I trust you to do this, I trust you not to do that—we introduce fragility

We can only trust people to do what they want to do, not what we want them to do.

into our relationship. If our partner steps over the lines we've drawn, even once, our relationship could collapse. *Real trust has no requirements.* It doesn't attempt to monitor, manipulate, or judge someone else's actions or behavior.

So what *can* we trust our partner to do? For one thing, we can trust them to behave in a manner that's consistent with their own beliefs and desires. We can trust them to make choices and decisions based on what they want. We can trust that whatever they do, it will be the best they can do at the time.

This kind of trust may seem scary at first, because we feel like we're not in control. But rather than making a relationship *fragile,* trust like this makes it *flexible*—and flexibility is strength. Just like buildings and bridges need flexibility to be able to withstand periods of extreme stress, relationships need flexibility to weather the unexpected.

Yvonne, who has this kind of trust in her husband, says, "Even if I sometimes wish Joshua had done something differently, I always believe that he made the best choice he could at the time—for me, for him, and for us—whatever that looks like. This makes our relationship feel much lighter and easier."

Yvonne recognizes that Joshua responds well to her "trust with no requirements." As he says, "I appreciate that Yvonne has such faith in me. It gives me a certain confidence knowing that she believes whatever I do will be the best thing."

In conjunction with trusting that everyone will act in alignment with their own beliefs and desires, here's something else you can put your trust in: *your own intuition.*

Intuition, which is knowing something without knowing exactly why you know it, is real. Our minds, which are more powerful than we can ever fully realize, take in and process millions of pieces of information and then communicate to us through what we call a gut feeling, a hunch, or our inner voice. Yet we often ignore or deny what that feeling or voice is trying to tell us.

Your inner wisdom deserves your trust. If you get an intuitive feeling that someone or something is unsafe or otherwise not right for you, learn to listen to and investigate that feeling.

Deanna, a successful artist in her mid-forties, has had several relationships with men who lied to her or hid things from her "in order to manipulate and control me, usually so I wouldn't break up with them." It took her years to realize, she says, "that I should always listen to my intuition and not stay too long in a relationship when I *know* intuitively that something is really wrong."

> **The more we learn to trust our intuition, the better our decisions will be and the more confident we'll feel.**

Set the Kind of Boundaries That Work

People are often advised to establish boundaries in their relation-ships, especially if they've been hurt before. As with trust, though, when we try to erect boundaries for someone else, we may be setting ourselves up for disappointment because we will never have control over what someone else does.

So what kind of boundaries *are* effective? The boundaries we set for *ourselves*. Boundaries like "I treat my body with love" and "I take care of myself" might mean we make sure to get enough exercise or make time for ourselves. They could also mean we won't allow our-selves to date someone who doesn't treat us well. For some people, establishing such boundaries might be the inspiration they need to begin taking steps to free themselves from an abusive situation.

Ann has these kinds of boundaries for herself. "In every relationship I'm in, I'm responsible for taking care of myself," she says. "This means I always act in a way that honors who I am and what's best for me."

ELEVATE YOUR APPRECIATION

Gratitude is the feeling of thankfulness that comes from recogniz-ing that you've received something of value, like the experience of beauty you get from watching a sunset. We naturally feel grateful when something special happens to us or when we recognize the wonderful things in our lives.

Making a conscious effort to feel genuine gratitude more often will have a profound effect on your life. Simply raising your *awareness* of all that's good in your life will increase your *experience* of good in your life. Gratitude helps you enjoy what you have instead of always looking for what's next.

Studies confirm that the more we feel gratitude for our partner and the more often we express it, the better both of us will feel about the relationship. To bring the power

> Focusing on
> what you have,
> rather than on
> what you don't,
> instantly
> makes your life
> feel fuller.

of gratitude into your relationship, simply take a little more notice of who your partner is and all he or she does for you. Tune in to your appreciation for the simple pleasure of their company when you're together. When you wear a shirt they've washed or use an appliance they've repaired, focus for a moment on your gratitude for that small act. From time to time, spend a few minutes contemplating all the contributions they've made to your life. Also make it a practice to express your gratitude more often. *Expressing your gratitude increases your awareness of what's wonderful in your life.*

Here's an even more powerful way to create a truly happy relationship experience: Cultivate appreciation for all aspects of your relationship, *including the challenging things your partner brings you to work with.* It's often through these challenges that we grow the most.

Stephanie, a tax accountant, met Sean the day she turned thirty. "Five months after we fell in love," she says, "he confessed that he was forty thousand dollars in debt."

At first, Stephanie thought about ending the relationship. "In the past, I would have done just that. I had this belief that anyone I dated had to be financially responsible." But Stephanie really loved being with Sean. They connected in every way that was important to her, and they could talk about anything.

"I decided to see what I could get out of being in relationship with someone who didn't have it all together financially," she says. "I learned there was plenty. For one thing, we spent a lot of time just being together instead of always looking for something to 'do.' We made love more often than I had in other relationships. And by helping Sean find his way through his money troubles, I actually feel stronger and more financially confident than ever before."

Making a conscious choice to appreciate what at first appears to be a difficult, negative, or "bad" situation is a skill you can develop through practice—and life will give you plenty of opportunities to practice! Developing this skill will allow you to experience more happiness in your life each and every day.

When you and your partner hold each other as guests in your lives, you give yourselves—and your relationship—essential space to breathe and to grow. Having that space makes it easier for you not only to weather the inevitable changes and challenges that arise, but to welcome them as opportunities to expand yourselves and your relationship.

6

Creating a Context

A context is a statement of what you intend to offer your
relationship. By pointing you toward higher possibilities,
your context will be your guide not only when your relationship
is feeling healthy and strong, but also when you're facing your
greatest challenges. A context will nourish and support
your relationship as it adapts to changing circumstances
and expands in new directions.

Kate and Nathan had plans for a romantic weekend away. On Thursday evening, Kate, thinking they'd decided to leave after work on Friday, mentioned that she'd arranged a business meeting for the following afternoon. Nathan was upset by this news, as he thought they'd agreed to leave first thing in the morning. He dreaded the idea of hitting the heavy afternoon traffic. To make matters worse, he felt the day would now be a waste because he purposely hadn't scheduled any clients.

The couple argued that evening, and Nathan spent all day Friday—as well as most of the four-hour drive to the mountains—feeling irritated and resentful.

Imagine how the couple's experience might have been different, however, if Nathan had approached the situation with this idea in mind: "My goal in this relationship is to make the most of every experience we have."

Having this context, or conscious intention, for their relationship may have led to an enlightening conversation (instead of an argument) about their different memories of their plans. Through this conversation, the couple might have come to the invaluable understanding that there is never one "right" version of what happens and that each person's perspective on any event is what is true for them.

With the context "My goal in this relationship is to make the most of every experience we have," Nathan might have initially felt disappointed about missing his opportunity to earn some income that day, but his attitude would probably have shifted quickly. He might have taken advantage of the unexpected free time to do some promotional work for his business. Or he could have started his vacation early by treating himself to something he wouldn't normally take the time for, like going mountain biking or checking out the new music store in town.

And the four-hour drive? Nathan would have been more relaxed and could have truly enjoyed his time with Kate—which was the whole purpose of their trip.

WHY ARE WE IN THIS RELATIONSHIP, ANYWAY?

We often go into a relationship without fully knowing why. Yes, we've met someone we're attracted to, we love spending time together, and we're feeling really good about ourselves. But then what?

When they're asked, many people say they want a relationship for intimacy or companionship. For others, it may be about being part of a family. But all too often, being in a relationship is really about need fulfillment. It's a common belief that our partner, by virtue of being in a relationship with us, is obligated to fulfill many of our outstanding needs.

It's easy to get a sense of this by checking out the ads on any dating site. You'll quickly learn what people are typically looking for in a relationship. Take a look at this actual ad:

Hello dear lover.

I love knowing I can count on you. You say what you mean and mean what you say.

I trust you and appreciate your generosity.

I love receiving your massages.

I love your powerful, gentle and respectful energy.

Can you relate? Then please respond with a photo.

On the surface, this woman seems to have a lot to offer. She appears positive and upbeat (she uses the word "love" three times), imaginative (her ad stands out from others), and comfortable in her body (she mentions massage, after all). But on closer reading, we discover that her primary interest is in what a prospective partner can do for *her*. We might even rewrite the ad in terms of her implied relationship requirements:

> Hello dear need-fulfiller.
> I feel secure knowing I can count on you to do what I expect you to do.
> I trust you to stay in line and to give me what I want.
> I'm happy you're here to satisfy my physical needs.
> I feel safe knowing that you will take care of me and won't disappoint me.
> Can you relate? Then send a photo so that I can judge your physical appearance.

It is possible that this ad will catch the attention of someone who's been looking for a woman with this exact set of expectations. It's more likely, though, that the people who respond will stick around only until they feel the expectation pressure start to build.

Now suppose the ad had been written by someone searching for a relationship based on ideas such as freedom, growth, and gratitude rather than on need fulfillment. It might come out something like this:

> Hello dear lover.
> I love knowing that we can always count on each other to be exactly who we are.
> I trust us to put every experience we have to its best possible use.
> I love exploring physical intimacy with you.
> I honor and appreciate that you are a multidimensional individual.
> If you can relate, I'd love to hear from you.

If you really want to create a soulmate experience, it's essential to examine the reasons why you are in a relationship or are looking for one. It can be revealing to write down exactly what you hope to get from a relationship. Once you've made your list, review it to see if there are any indications of things you believe you need from a partner or any sense of "I wouldn't be happy if he or she didn't have this or give me that."

The definition
of a soulmate
is not
"someone who fulfills
all your needs."

Every requirement you have cuts down on the possibilities for connection. In fact, *the more requirements you have for a relationship, the more difficult it will be to create and sustain a soulmate experience.* So rather than focusing on what you *want* from a relationship, it's time to turn your attention to what you can *offer* one.

WHAT IS A RELATIONSHIP CONTEXT?

The belief that a relationship is a fifty-fifty proposition is sure to lead to a great deal of frustration. Each one of us brings different strengths, passions, and abilities to a relationship. We all have areas in which we can naturally and easily contribute more than our partner. In some areas, we might contribute 80 percent to our partner's 20 percent; in others, our roles could be reversed. Many couples grow frustrated trying to evenly split all their shared responsibilities, such as household chores, financial matters, or making progress toward shared goals.

A more effective way to approach a relationship is through the idea of context. *A context is a personal declaration of what you intend to contribute to your relationship.*

Why would you want to make such a declaration? Because if you don't have a conscious context for your relationship, you'll end up with an unconscious one.

A typical unconscious context might be "I'm performing my roles as husband, father, and income producer because that's what I'm expected to do." Though this man's family may be comfortably provided for, a context like this may eventually result in a relationship that is characterized by anxiety, resignation, or even depression. Similarly, a context like "I'm here because I made a commitment to be here" may in time produce a relationship characterized by boredom, drudgery, or resentment.

> The true guiding light in a relationship isn't the promises you made at the beginning. It's the intentions you operate with each and every day.

Another common unconscious context is some version of "I'm here to be taken care of" or "What's in it for me?" A context like this has the potential to turn every encounter between two people into a struggle. These relationships can involve arguments and compromises as partners jockey to get whatever they can. As time goes on, they often become filled with frustration, disappointment, anger, or regret.

You can see that unconscious contexts often lead to feelings of alienation. Conscious relationship contexts, on the other hand, can lead to greater connection. Take a look at these three actual contexts:

- "I nurture our relationship to ensure we preserve this very special thing we have."

- "I bring inspiration and motivation to our relationship to keep it exciting and alive."

- "I believe that everything in our relationship will serve us in some way."

Elizabeth, a therapist, holds this last context for her marriage. When something comes up that initially feels difficult, her context offers her guidance. "I may not know *how* something is going to serve us until much later," she says, "but just knowing that it *will* serve us is a big help. Things seem to flow much more easily that way."

Dean, who's been married twelve years, says, "I always wondered why people treat each other the way they do in marriages. When they're dating, they want the other person to want them. Later on, when they feel confident that person won't leave them, they stop trying to make themselves wanted." With this in mind, Dean took on a context when he married Jennifer. He says, "I decided to try to always behave as if I want to be wanted. This mindset has helped me to make an effort in the relationship: to appreciate Jennifer, treat her with respect, and always be open to who she is."

Evan and Leanne have been married several years. At some point, Evan began to realize that he'd become very needy. He spent a lot of time directing low-level blame at Leanne, and he often felt mildly resentful about not getting everything he thought he should. He decided that a significant contribution he could make to his relationship would be to take responsibility for himself. He stated his new context as "I am fully responsible for getting my own needs met."

To Evan's surprise, he discovered that his new approach to his relationship immediately made him feel more capable and empowered. "It felt great not to be constantly trying to manipulate Leanne into doing things for me and then blaming her in my mind when she didn't get the hint," he says.

And Leanne? "Without even knowing what Evan was up to, I instantly felt lighter," she reports. "Like some invisible weight had been lifted from me."

Do you remember Elaine from Chapter 5, whose boyfriend isn't as sexually assertive as Elaine would like? Jordan is always a willing participant, and he frequently tells Elaine how beautiful and sexy he finds her. But he rarely initiates sexual contact.

If Elaine could accept that Jordan simply isn't wired like she is, she could then decide to take on the role of keeping their connection sexually vibrant. After all, she has that ability in abundance! This would, of course, require her to give up the idea that if Jordan doesn't come on to her, it means he doesn't find her desirable. In essence, Elaine would have to let go of the belief that Jordan's lack of sex drive means something about her value.

> Having a context creates an environment for a relationship to thrive.

CREATING A CONTEXT

Suppose Elaine took on this context: "I bring to this relationship my desire to keep sex fun and exciting." Such an intention might inspire her to come up with sexy games to play, make arrangements for a romantic weekend, or sign them up for a couples' tantra workshop. Any of these possibilities would be more fun and inspiring than the alternative: growing more and more distant from and resentful of Jordan over time.

Although applying this context would require continued effort and attention on Elaine's part, if she is happy with the relationship overall, she may find that it's well worthwhile to contribute more than Jordan in this area. A context like "I bring to this relationship my desire to keep sex fun and exciting" may seem unusual, but if this is the one area that someone feels is lacking, making this contribution has the potential to transform a good relationship into an extraordinary one.

A CONTEXT POINTS YOU TOWARD
A HIGHER POSSIBILITY

Michael Naumer defined context as "a declaration of a higher possibility for your relationship." He said, "A context is a *star* that you can guide your relationship by. Without that guiding star, your relationship compass just spins round and round."

Having a context in place can be invaluable for addressing the most challenging issues that arise in relationships, including money, our partner's habits, and emotionally charged situations.

Money

One problematic area in many relationships is money. A context can help you remain clear about your priorities when financial issues arise, as well as lessen the fears that often accompany such issues.

Lee is a painter and a photographer; her partner, Sondra, is a writer. Lee and Sondra share a context for their relationship: "Our relationship is a place where we can both develop our gifts and give back to our community." When a financial issue comes up, they find their context helpful in guiding their decision making. For example, they decided to eat out less often in order to be able to afford to take more workshops and art classes. When it came to prioritizing the home improvement projects on their wish list, they opted for converting their garage into a creative workspace instead of adding a second bathroom to their home.

Our Partner's Habits

A context can also offer direction when you find yourself annoyed with something your significant other is doing. After her boyfriend, Kyle, moved in, Tara discovered that he was much less attentive to housekeeping details than she was. He'd leave cupboards open, put the phone down in odd places, and splash water on the counter when he shaved.

The conventional relationship advice in such a situation would be to communicate and compromise. You'd talk about the problem, express your feelings honestly, listen to your partner's perspective, and then negotiate a mutual agreement about how to address the issue. In their situation, Kyle and Tara might reach a compromise like

"I agree to try to remember to put the cap on the toothpaste, and you agree to try not to get upset when I forget."

On the surface, this may seem like a great solution. *But filling a relationship with agreements like these is like filling it with landmines.* Eventually, you're going to step on one. Kyle would no doubt forget to put the cap on the toothpaste from time to time, potentially resulting in frustration on Tara's part and guilt on his.

Tara, however, had planned ahead. She'd established a context for her relationship with Kyle before he'd moved in: "I use everything that happens to bring us closer together." She knew that these sorts of little habits were a common issue in sharing a household. She also knew that even if she and Kyle communicated about them openly and honestly, his habits still had the potential to be an ongoing source of irritation between them. So, she explains, "Rather than mentioning them at all, I decided to see them as reminders of having this incredible person in my life."

When disagreements arise, turn to your context to guide you toward a higher possibility.

As she practiced this, she discovered that Kyle's forgetfulness bothered her less and less. A few months later, she felt the desire to share with Kyle how successful she'd been in shifting her experience. He was so impressed that she'd never once mentioned any of his oversights that he was inspired to become more aware of his own habits. "He's even asked me to remind him when he forgets!" Tara says with a smile.

Do you remember Evan, who took on the context "I am fully responsible for getting my own needs met"? Soon after he'd declared this context, his wife took a new job. The position required her to get up two hours earlier than she had before. At first, Evan was annoyed at being woken up every morning at four o'clock. "I'd lie there thinking, 'I'll never get back to sleep!'"

After two frustrating weeks, Evan remembered to apply his new context to the situation. "I realized there were actually options for me. I could use those early morning hours to get up and stretch or plan out my day. Or I could change my work schedule to better match hers." When he started looking at these other possibilities, he reported, "The resentment I was feeling just went away."

Emotionally Charged Situations

Contexts are also invaluable for addressing situations that could easily be perceived as threatening to our relationship.

Rebecca and Jacob each have a context for their relationship. Jacob's is "We're in this together." Rebecca's is "I make our relationship a place for transformation and joy."

Jacob tells a story about a yoga teacher at the gym where he works out. "We've said hi a few times, and I've talked to her about taking her class. Then one day after my workout, I found her business card on my bag—with 'Call me sometime' written on the back!"

Jacob found himself amused and flattered, as well as a little nervous. "With my previous girlfriends, I would have told the woman I wasn't interested and just kept quiet about the whole thing. But even though I didn't know what Rebecca's reaction would be, 'We're in this together' made me want to share it with her instead."

When Jacob told her the story, Rebecca admits, "Although I know this kind of stuff happens, I was still a little shocked. But Jacob helped me to understand that he really was coming from 'We're in this together,' and that made me feel loved."

That feeling of being loved gave Rebecca encouragement to look at the situation through her own context of making their relationship a place for transformation and joy.

"The first realization I came to was that this was a chance for me to respond out of something other than jealousy or suspicion," she says. "So I actually suggested we go take her yoga class together! And instead of feeling like I needed to check out my competition, as I would have in the past, I felt I was a part of Jacob's experience somehow."

"It was amazing," Jacob says. "Rebecca treated this like an interesting life event that we could share together, rather than something to be afraid of. She actually told Lori that she admired her for having such courage! And I'm so grateful not to have to hide things like this from her."

It may be hard to imagine that two people can grow more connected through an experience that would typically produce feelings of separation or fear. But when you use your context a few times in the face of challenging circumstances like these, you'll discover how truly powerful it is. It will be there for you every time you could use a reminder of the reasons why you're in this relationship.

WHY CONTEXT CAN BE
MORE POWERFUL THAN COMMITMENT

We have many different ideas about what the word "commitment" means when it's applied to relationships. In conventional relationships, it's often defined in one of these ways:

- "Commitment means you always keep your promises, no matter what."

- "Commitment means you put the other person's needs ahead of your own."

- "Commitment means you focus all of your sexual thoughts and energy on your partner."

- "Commitment means that no matter what happens, even if you fall out of love, you will stay together."

At first glance, these ideas may seem like they would create a supportive foundation for a relationship. But look more closely and you'll notice that, in part, these definitions of commitment are all attempts to cement certain guarantees from a partner. We often do this to decrease our feelings of fear, like the fear of abandonment, of not being special, or of not having things go our way.

Defining our relationship through commitments like these has the potential to entangle us in a sticky web of rules and expectations. It's no wonder that many people are afraid that committing to a relationship means they'll face the loss of individuality and freedom.

At its core, true commitment isn't about defining what you or your partner should or should not do. *True commitment is a personal act of intention, of declaring to yourself, "I intend for this to work."* Rather than pro-ducing expectations, a commitment like this—like a context for your relationship—produces *possibilities.*

CREATING YOUR CONTEXT

While you've been reading this, you might have been thinking about crafting your own relationship context. Create your context when you're feeling clear and grounded, so that it will contain your great-est wisdom. You might begin by asking yourself these questions: *Is there anything I've been wanting more of in this relationship that I could decide to be responsible for providing? Is there anything that seems to be lacking that I could bring into this relationship with the power of my intention?*

When you're developing your context, you want it to be some-thing that feels possible for you. You want to be able to say, "Yes, I can do this. I have the ability to choose this on a day-to-day basis."

For example, a context like "I am unconditionally loving all the time" is not realistic for most of us right now. "I am open to people's souls" may not be very practical in the heat of the moment. Instead, you might try something like "I provide a safe and loving space for our relationship."

Next, your context should be clear and concise, yet broad enough to apply to a variety of situations. You want it to be easily accessible when you're facing something that could be challenging to your relationship.

This will take some thought. A broad statement like "I bring inspiration, fun, trust, intimacy, and support to our relationship" may sound like it covers all the bases. But because there's so much to remember, it would be difficult to apply when things get bumpy. "I bring warmth and intimacy to our relationship," on the other hand, is expansive enough to offer intelligent guidance in many kinds of circumstances, and is focused enough to be easily remembered and applied.

> Your context
> gives you access
> to your own highest wisdom
> at those times when
> you most need it.

Finally, your context should point you in the direction of greater love, intimacy, and connection.

Your Context Will Evolve as You Do

As you experiment with your context and apply it to different areas of your life, you may discover that it changes or evolves. Evan, for example, who has the context "I am fully responsible for getting my own needs met," might one day find he has integrated that wisdom into who he is and no longer needs to consciously remind himself of it. He might then create a new context to make his relationship experience even more rewarding.

You may also discover that you'd like to fine-tune your context. While called away for military duty overseas, separated from his wife and children, Patrick came to this understanding: "Family is the most important thing." He was determined that when he returned home, this context would be his guiding principle every day. If something didn't directly support his context, he wouldn't even consider it.

A few years later, though, Patrick found himself increasingly anxious and stressed. He'd gained weight. He felt stiff, weak, and tired a lot of the time. He knew he needed to exercise, but between his work and family responsibilities, he didn't feel it was possible to carve out any time for himself. The context "Family is the most important thing" was actually preventing him from addressing his own needs.

To find balance in his life, Patrick needed to recognize that a family is at its healthiest when every individual has the opportunity to develop into their best possible self. Patrick was doing everything in his power to make this a possibility for his wife and children, but was neglecting himself in the process. He needed to be reminded that if he also takes care of himself, he will be better able to nurture, support, and enjoy his family. A broader, more expansive context like "I create an environment for *all* of us to be our very best selves" might be more effective. Patrick will probably discover that when he takes the time to exercise regularly, providing for his family will be easier and more rewarding.

Complementary Contexts

When two people develop their individual contexts for their relationship, they often find that those contexts naturally go well together. This makes sense, as we are often drawn to people who have strengths that complement ours.

Katie, who teaches elementary school, takes painting and sculpting classes and always has several art projects in the works at home. Her husband, Todd, is a tax accountant whose favorite pastimes are gardening and reading.

Todd, the more grounded of the two, holds the space for their relationship to thrive. His context is "I create a safe environment so we both feel supported and loved." This context nurtures their relationship so that it continues to develop and flourish.

Context is essentially this: I offer the best of me; you offer the best of you.

Katie, who is more adventurous, holds the possibility for making life stimulating. Her context is "I bring inspiration to our relationship to keep it playful and exciting." This context energizes their relationship so that it continues to feel vibrant.

Speaking about Todd's context, Katie says, "He helps create a perfect environment for me to explore my creative side, which is so important to me." And Todd says of Katie's context, "I never imagined that someone would be willing to step up and make a relationship as fun as she does!"

Shared Contexts

People in soulmate relationships often report that they have a higher purpose for being together. This is something that goes beyond the usual reasons like intimacy or companionship. Some couples are committed to a charitable, humanitarian, or ecological cause, or to raising their children in a conscious, loving environment in the hopes that they will grow up to make positive contributions to their community. Others devote their partnership to a more personal endeavor, such as learning to be more compassionate toward everyone they encounter.

If you and your partner feel that you have a higher purpose for being together but haven't put it into words, or if you haven't ever considered what your relationship's higher purpose might be, you may want to explore the idea. Consider this question: *Is there something we're both passionate about that we could contribute to the world—and, in the process, enhance our own relationship?*

Creating a shared context will not only enrich your relationship but also deepen the connection you experience every day. Having a higher purpose gives you and your partner a truly worthwhile reason to be together.

Creating a context for your relationship will allow you to apply your own highest wisdom in the midst of your most difficult moments. It will enable you to see higher possibilities in every challenge that comes along. In a similar way, designing a shared context will give your relationship meaning and direction, keeping your partnership on course and always moving toward greater love, intimacy, and connection.

7

Making Space

*Like every living thing, your relationship needs space to
grow, develop, and stay healthy. A safe, loving, supportive
environment allows you and your partner to sustain your love
and deepen your intimacy as you expand yourselves and
make the most of all your experiences together.*

Most of us did not have the luxury of growing up in an environment where we felt completely free to be ourselves. At home, in school and places of worship, and even with our closest friends, we learned there were things that were best kept hidden. Some of us were taught to keep our emotions to ourselves or to stay quiet about our talents and accomplishments. By a very young age, many of us knew not to reveal certain things we had done (or even thought) or risk being emotionally or physically punished.

The nuns at the Catholic school Jim attended told him daily that by virtue of being a boy, he was trouble and required constant watching. Colleen, who also went to parochial school, learned early on that if she showed curiosity about her body, she wasn't being a "good girl" in the eyes of God.

Because his father held a firm belief that "big boys don't cry," Javier struggled to keep himself from feeling emotions that might lead to tears. In Denesha's family, ridicule was a daily experience. She learned never to reveal anything remotely personal, knowing it could, and probably would, be used against her.

Although our teachers and parents were doing the best they knew how, they communicated in many ways that it was not acceptable or safe for us to be ourselves.

A SAFE, LOVING SPACE
MAKES TRUE INTIMACY POSSIBLE

In many workshops and discussion groups, people have an opportunity to share intimate details about themselves and their lives. These groups are most beneficial when an environment of trust is created in which the participants agree that what is said in the group will not be repeated outside of the group. When people feel safe to reveal themselves, they can gain valuable insight into their emotions, motivations, and behavior. They may even be able to release painful experiences and beliefs that they've been holding onto for years.

Counselors and therapists understand that a safe, loving environment is essential for experiencing true connection in our relationships. They know that real intimacy involves exposing ourselves: bringing our deepest thoughts, feelings, and desires out into the open. We are only drawn to be this revealing when we know we're in a caring, supportive environment.

When we are able to be our authentic self with our significant other, we can talk about what's really going on for us, even about things many couples find frightening or taboo. Bringing the darkest parts of ourselves into the light, in the presence of our partner, bonds us at a level of intimacy beyond what most couples experience. It's that bond that will enable us to accept and even embrace the most challenging of circumstances we might encounter together.

In addition to fostering true intimacy, a safe, loving relationship space encourages us to continually expand ourselves. When we are young, it's natural to experiment: acquiring new skills, testing our limitations, and trying out new ways of being. As adults, it's equally natural to continue this self-exploration: developing our interests and talents, welcoming new ideas and people, and inquiring into the meaning and purpose of our lives. However, many of us have inadvertently shut the doors to this process of self-discovery. Having experienced judgment, rejection, and "failure" in the past, we believe others won't love or approve of us if they see who we really are.

> When you do your best to embrace everything your partner brings forward, they will be more drawn to you than ever.

Once we create a safe space, we'll be inspired to throw those closed doors wide open. When we know our partner truly accepts us, we'll be more creative and playful and much more willing to take risks. We'll be drawn to connect with new people and receptive to new possibilities. We'll be inclined to say yes when we used to say no.

Just as children who are raised in a loving, supportive environment carry their confidence out into the world, a loving partnership space supports us even when we're on our own. We'll be more likely to try something new, as we know there's a willing, receptive audience to share our experiences with later. Whether these experiences are exhilarating, challenging, or even discouraging, we know our partner will be there to help us learn all we can from them.

CLEAR THE SPACE
BY RELEASING YOUR RESENTMENTS

We make a safe, loving space for our relationships by learning to fully embrace our partner, ourselves, and everything that shows up. *In essence, we create a safe space through acceptance.*

What do you get when you accept each other completely, or even close to completely? You get what every relationship requires in order to thrive: *freedom.* When you aren't spending your time and energy resisting who your partner is or what they're doing—when you can really *be* there when you're with them—then you're free to enjoy and appreciate all that your partner and your relationship have to offer.

As you enter a new relationship, make a commitment to do whatever is necessary to create and maintain a safe, loving relationship space. Yes, this will require intention and determination. But it's far more rewarding—and certainly easier—than untangling the mess we usually create through months or years of unconscious relating.

If you've been in a relationship for a while and layers of resentment and distrust have built up, it will take
a committed effort from both of you to create a loving, supportive environment. Every
step you take in this direction, though, will
increase the possibility of experiencing true
intimacy and joy in your relationship.

**A safe relationship
space is free of
judgment,
criticism, and blame.**

We often insist we can't let go of things we find irritating or feel
resentful about. But this idea is only another limiting belief. When
we finally realize that what we're holding onto is the real cause of
our suffering—*and when our desire for connection is stronger than our desire to
be right*—we really *can* just drop it. To create and sustain a soulmate
experience, it's essential that we learn to be flexible when we realize
we have positions, expectations, or other attachments to how things
should be.

Identify Your Resentments

A powerful way to free your relationship from the suffocating burden
of resentments is to dissolve them *together*. If you are both committed to creating a loving, safe relationship space, then bringing your
resentments out into the open and helping each other find ways to
release them can be an incredibly bonding experience.

If you want to try this together, know that it will take a strong
intention to stay connected as you focus on releasing, and thereby
healing, your resentments. The pull to get drawn back in to defending

and justifying your position may be quite strong. Stay with the process only as long as you both feel it's helpful—meaning as long as it's *decreasing* resentment rather than *increasing* it!

> We're unlikely to get relationship satisfaction through the belief that it's our partner who has to change.

If you're not ready to try this process as a couple, doing it on your own is equally valuable. Each resentment you let go of will immediately bring more space and harmony into your life and into your relationship experience.

Begin this process by taking a personal inventory. Make a list of any resentments you hold toward your partner. These might be about things from the past, like "You didn't give me a party on my thirtieth birthday." Or they could be about situations that come up on a regular basis, such as "I get irritated when you leave dishes on the counter."

Once you've identified everything you can, prioritize the items on your list according to which you think will be the easiest to let go of.

Dissolve Your Resentments One by One

If you've agreed to try this process together, begin by experimenting with little things that don't matter much to either of you. Share one of your resentments and, together, look for ways to release it.

To the best of your ability, be open-minded and objective as you do this. Viewing your resentments, and your partner's, as though they belong to someone else is one way to keep from getting emotionally caught up in them. Remember, the idea here is to use your partner's support—which is often just their loving presence—to let go of your resentments, not to try to change your partner.

If you're doing this on your own and feel your partner would be receptive, you might share with him or her that you're in the process of uncovering and releasing your resentments.

To begin the purging process, remind yourself that your resentments are choices you're making about how you see or relate to your partner and that *you can choose differently.* Then examine your resentments one by one. For each one, ask yourself these questions:

- Will holding this resentment help me to create a relationship that is loving and connected?

- Am I willing to accept what I've been resenting in order to have a more fulfilling relationship experience?

- Is it possible that someone else could easily accept this about my partner?

Now turn to the lenses described in "Free Yourself from Resentment" in Chapter 3. For each resentment on your list, see if one of these lenses will help you begin to dissolve it.

If you're doing this as a couple, you might say something like, "I realize I get resentful when you say you'll be home at six and you get home at seven. I don't want to have that experience any more." Then you might explore together what the situation would look like if seen through the "this isn't about my value" lens or the "everyone is doing the best they can" lens.

As you begin to release yourself from the weight of your positions and attachments, you will feel your relationship opening up. In this freer, lighter space, you'll naturally relate to each other with more expansive, receptive attitudes.

While her fiancé was away on a bachelor's weekend three weeks before their wedding, Avasa devoted some time to assessing the resentments she'd accumulated over their two-year relationship. The first one she investigated was her resentment over the amount of time Matt liked to spend watching movies. She usually joined him, though often feeling mildly resentful that they weren't doing something she felt would be more meaningful.

Avasa recognized that she'd been interpreting the time Matt spent watching movies as time he wasn't giving her attention, and equating this to a lack of love for her. She could see that her resistance in this area hadn't brought them closer together—in fact, the opposite was true.

Even though she may not fully understand it, she realized, this pastime is how Matt recharges. It occurred to her that she could use his movie-watching time as an opportunity to recharge herself. While he relaxed in front of the screen, she could take a bath, read, write in her journal, or do any of a number of things she'd been having trouble finding time for.

The night Matt returned from his weekend away, Avasa was feeling light and energized and very excited to see him. After giving her

> It takes precious life energy to maintain resentments— energy that will be available for other purposes when we choose to accept rather than to resist.

a big hug and kiss, the first thing Matt said was, "I'm really exhausted. I'd love to just get a video tonight."

"Okay," Avasa said with a smile—and was immediately rewarded with her fiancé's amused look of surprise. By releasing the resentment she'd been carrying, Avasa reports, "I'm a new woman. Everything is *so* much easier!"

Avasa's newfound ability to shift her perspective is a gift to their upcoming marriage, one that has the power to prevent minor issues from becoming major issues. If her resentment comes up again, she'll recognize it—and she'll know how to transform it into something positive for both of them.

KEEPING YOUR RELATIONSHIP SPACE CLEAN

Most couples consider many of the things that arise in their relationship too trivial to address. But left unattended, that "trivial" stuff—such as minor grievances or unspoken expectations about our significant other or our relationship—collects into larger issues, until one day we may find ourselves overwhelmed by the thought of untangling ourselves from them.

If you and your partner have created a safe, loving environment for your relationship, it will be easy to notice when even the smallest stuff shows up in it. *To keep your relationship space clean, address issues as they arise.*

"That sounds like too much work," people often protest. "Can't we just agree to let some things go?"

The problem is, most of us don't really know *how* to let things go. What we do instead is try to ignore or cover up our feelings of irritation, resentment, and hurt in the hopes they'll eventually go away.

Of course, these feelings don't just go away—and the more of this stuff we accumulate, the less clarity we have to deal with new challenges that arise. With a jumble of unresolved issues, we often have difficulty sorting out what's upsetting us when something else crops up. That's because *new feelings of resentment, anger, or irritation will often trigger similar emotions still lingering in us from the past.* You can see this when couples argue. They start with one topic and then begin to dredge up past resentments and throw those into the ring as well.

> By not allowing things to accumulate in your relationship space, you make room for other possibilities.

By resolving issues as they come up, our relationship remains a place where we both want to be.

WHEN THINGS SHOW UP
—AND THEY WILL!

The secret to addressing challenges as they come up is to approach them in a way that makes every issue resolvable and, at the same time, enhances your connection with your partner.

Despite what we might hear about compromise being the best way to resolve issues, it doesn't always result in a stronger bond between two people. By definition, compromise means "to adjust or settle by mutual concessions." It may involve making agreements about how you and your partner will act or behave, establishing new rules, or putting other limitations or restrictions into place.

Though rules and restrictions may give us a temporary sense of security, they rarely strengthen a relationship. In fact, as they accumulate, they can severely weaken it. In addition, such limitations are often accompanied by guilt and resentment. When we compromise, we're essentially saying, "I agree to be less and less of who I am, and you agree to be less and less of who you are." In the process, we slowly choke off our relationship's capacity for growth, self-expression, and joy.

The practice of acceptance, rather than compromise, is the shortest path to an open, expansive experience with your partner.

When one of you realizes that there's some feeling of separation between you, take a breath. Remind yourselves that this is an opportunity to increase your connection. In fact, it's the perfect opportunity—because *every challenge in your relationship has the potential to lead both of you toward deeper intimacy.* The first person who summons the self-awareness to notice the separation can lead the two of you in a more harmonious direction. The need to be right is often fierce, so this can take some willpower. Gently call attention to the disconnect without making either of you feel at fault for it. This will offer you both a chance to step away from your positions (not away from each other!) and see the situation from a broader perspective. You might say something like, "Hey, sweetie, I sense we're both

> **Every challenge in your relationship is perfect for your growth— and your partner's.**

feeling the need to be right. How about we break from this conversation for a moment and take a look at what's really going on for us?"

The key now is to use the opening you've created to shift your
attention away from the immediate issue. You may both need some
time to check in with yourselves. Allow yourselves to feel the emotions that have been stirred up in you. However, don't energize them
by continuing to think about the issue in an oppositional way, such
as how best to convince your partner of your position. The urge to
be right may influence you for a while longer, but you can always
choose not to act on it.

From this more expansive perspective, check in to see if you're
both ready to talk about your experience without reengaging over
the issue. By making a conscious decision to let go of your positions
as much as possible, you can explore the
situation from a place of togetherness
rather than from a place of separation.
In the receptive space this creates,
you're more likely to be able to acknowledge and accept any thoughts, feelings,
or reactions either of you expresses,
without finger-pointing or blame.

> We don't
> need to improve
> our communication skills
> so much as we
> need to be aware of
> the *intention*
> with which
> we're communicating.

Accepting whatever your partner brings forward doesn't imply agreement, and it isn't about allowing your partner to walk all over you.
*It simply means you recognize and honor that this is your partner's experience at
this moment.*

Bring forward anything new that you become aware of in the

process of this exploration. "I see I'm still wanting to be right about this—there's a part of me that doesn't want to let this go." "I'm realizing that I'm worried you won't like me if you know this about me."

If the urge to accuse arises in you, simply acknowledge it in a nonthreatening way: "I'm noticing that I'm wanting to blame you for this." If your partner says something like this to you, accept this as their experience at the moment. "I can understand that," you might say. "I've been there too."

Now it's time to discover what it is that each of you has "outside your circle."

EXPAND TO INCLUDE
AND HAVE IT CONTRIBUTE

Imagine drawing a circle around yourself. All the things you accept in your life—people, situations, ideas—are inside that circle. Everything else, whatever you're resisting, is outside that circle.

"When you're suffering," Michael Naumer often said, "it's because there's something outside your circle. Whatever you've got outside your circle runs you and runs your relationship."

Maintaining your resistance to things outside your circle requires a lot of energy. For example, if you haven't accepted the fact that your significant other isn't as neat as you are, you will frequently find yourself irritated by his or her untidiness. If they have a habit you find annoying—like a loud laugh, or a sound they make when they eat—you'll probably be distracted when you're with them, unable to be completely comfortable. Such resistance takes energy that you could be putting to better uses.

When you and your partner are investigating anything that's come up between you, your goal is to discover what it is that's outside your circle. This is something you aren't seeing, acknowledging, or accepting about your partner, yourself, or the situation. It's often a belief or an assumption that isn't serving you, and it will usually be different for each of you.

Once you find what's outside your circle, you're looking at the true cause of your disharmony. You now have the opportunity, as Christina Naumer, Michael Naumer's wife, phrased it, to "expand to include and have it contribute." *When you expand your circle to embrace what you've been rejecting and allow it to contribute to your experience, the issue you've been struggling with will begin to dissolve.*

Finding a way for something outside your circle to actually contribute may at first seem impossible. After all, sometimes we've been rejecting a situation or idea for years, all the while collecting evidence for why we should continue to reject it.

To get around our defenses, it helps to reflect on questions such as these: *What is there to appreciate about this being in my life? What opportunity is this situation presenting me? In what way could this situation actually contribute to my relationship?*

If you and your partner have different approaches to being in a relationship, "expand to include and have it contribute" will help you create a new approach that works for both of you.

138

Using "Expand to Include and Have It Contribute"

When Sophie and Jason first started dating, they were eager to be together whenever possible. But after a few months, they found themselves struggling with the question of just how much time to spend with each other.

Sophie is passionately involved in a number of projects and activities; Jason is more of the quiet type. While Jason appreciates that Sophie has many interests she's pursuing, he also feels it's important that couples do things together often.

The friction over the issue of how they divide their time peaked whenever Jason invited Sophie to an event like a baseball game or a car show. Sophie, torn between her projects and the desire to accommodate Jason, was frustrated by these invitations. She usually ended up going, but felt resentful about the time the outings were taking away from her own aspirations.

Unable to resolve this issue, Jason and Sophie agreed to take a look at it from a new perspective. Jason would search for whatever was outside his circle and expand to include that, and Sophie would do the same.

Sophie discovered what was outside her circle was the fact that Jason enjoys doing things with no goal in mind. At first she resisted the idea that such activities could contribute anything of value to their relationship. Then she asked herself, *What is there to appreciate about this being in my life?* She quickly recognized that she wouldn't necessarily *want* to be in a relationship with someone as driven as she is. She also realized that Jason's more grounded approach to life actually complemented her own very well, and she began to feel grateful for his calming influence.

Then Sophie considered this question: *In what way could this contribute to our relationship?* She decided that she could view Jason's invitations as an opportunity to recharge. If she felt that being with him would be beneficial, she would go—and with an intention to fully enjoy herself.

Jason saw that what was outside his circle was the idea that happy couples don't need to do things together all the time. "I'd always believed that *being together* was what a relationship was all about," he said.

When he asked himself, *What is there to appreciate about this being in my life?* Jason realized there were several ways that Sophie's lack of interest in the activities he enjoyed could contribute to their relationship. He could draw inspiration from her commitment to what was important to her. He could appreciate the fact that their relationship gave him plenty of free time to be with his sons, who love car shows and ball games. And he could use the time away from Sophie to increase his excitement about being with her when they *did* get together.

It may take a bit of searching to find a way for some things to contribute to your relationship. Consider Ben, a thirty-something athlete. He'd been dating Sarah for several months and was having a difficult time with the fact that she smokes.

"She only allows herself one cigarette a day," he said, "and never around me, but I'm uncomfortable that she's doing something so destructive to her body."

> Everything that arises in your relationship can be an opportunity to increase your connection.

Reluctantly, Ben agreed to consider the possibility that Sarah's smoking could actually make a contribution to their relationship. "One reason I resist it so much," he found, "is because I hope my disapproval will motivate her to quit!" But he could see he hadn't been a positive influence. On the contrary, his resistance had made Sarah resentful and withdrawn.

Ben then considered the question *What opportunity is this situation presenting me with?* He realized that this was the perfect chance to practice accepting other people's lifestyle choices—something he'd been working on for years. If he couldn't do this with the woman he loved, it would be very difficult to do with anyone else.

Within a few days, Ben discovered that he really could be just fine with Sarah's smoking. As often happens when we finally stop resisting what someone is doing, Ben also began to notice a change in Sarah. She was more relaxed around him. A few weeks later, she even mentioned that maybe it was time for her to give up smoking for good.

Ben had made an intriguing discovery. *While the practice of acceptance has nothing to do with whether or not someone else changes, it's surprising how often it has that effect.*

Play "Expand to Include" Together

You and your partner can even make a game of approaching challenging circumstances, situations, or people in a spirit of *What is there to appreciate about having this in our lives? What opportunity is this situation presenting us? How could this contribute to our relationship?* Search for something you're both bothered by, such as a grouchy neighbor or the crowded parking lot at the grocery store. Then experiment with new ways to view the situation that will allow you to expand your relationship circle to include this in it.

You can also play with the time lag between the occurrence of something unexpected and the moment when you find a way to accept and incorporate it. When the car breaks down, you miss your flight, or you get to the theater and find that tickets are sold out, how soon can one of you begin the shift away from frustration or disappointment toward a more positive response?

As you play "expand to include," you'll find that your circle continues to widen. *The wider your circle becomes, the more space you will have to sustain a healthy relationship.*

By creating a loving, supportive relationship space,
you and your partner will find yourselves relating on ever more
intimate levels. When challenges arise, you'll know that rather than
separating you, these moments can actually bring you closer together.
A safe space will also give you an opportunity to expand your
relationship in exciting new ways, because what you're
really creating is a space for higher possibilities.

8

Turning Expectations
into Invitations

Expectations may be the single greatest threat to experiencing true connection and harmony in your relationship. Before you're even aware of them, these beliefs about what your partner should or shouldn't do can inflict great damage. Beneath every expectation, though, is an authentic desire to connect with the person you love. When you express those authentic desires through simple invitations, everything in your relationship has the potential to show up as a gift.

W hen you first start seeing someone, you naturally present your very best self. It's more than just finding interesting things to do and making sure you don't have spinach in your teeth. You're likely to be receptive, energetic, and willing to try something new. You're open to who this person is and to seeing the world from his or her perspective.

Think back to when you were dating someone new. You're out to dinner, thoroughly enjoying the feeling of being in this special twosome. The food arrives, but you're so captivated by the conversation that you barely touch it.

The relationship develops, and weeks or months go by. You still enjoy being together, but now when you go out, you're often more focused on the menu and the food than on each other. Slowly and almost imperceptibly, relating has been overshadowed by the details of daily life.

What happened? How did your new relationship go from extraordinary one day to just plain ordinary the next?

A primary cause of this shutting-down process is the arising of expectations. *An expectation is a belief we hold about how another person should act or behave.* The truth is, most of us have a lot of them. Not surprisingly, it's often easier to recognize other people's expectations than to see our own.

Our expectations may begin to damage our relationship long before we realize that they're contributing to our problems or even that we have them. By the time we do become aware of our expectations, just contemplating what it would take to untangle ourselves from them can leave us feeling confused, overwhelmed, and depressed.

THE FALL FROM THE PEDESTAL

When you're in a new relationship, you feel like you're in a higher state of consciousness. Once the novelty has worn off, you may look back wistfully at that time. You might even tell yourself the magic you felt was all an illusion. But for that period of time, you really *were* in a higher state of consciousness. You were open to what this new relationship was all about and who you could be in it. You were willing to explore and to change. You accepted your new lover's personality traits, interests, and idiosyncrasies with a minimum of judgment.

Being open and accepting is precisely what a higher state of consciousness is.

Some people warn us not to put our new love on a pedestal. They caution that once we come down from our relationship high, the person we're holding in such a place of honor will tumble off the pedestal we've placed them on and we will experience yet another relationship letdown.

Unless our new lover has misrepresented themselves—such as telling us they're single when they're married—having them on a pedestal is a reflection of our *own* higher state. We've put them there by being open to them—emotionally, physically, and psychologically—and receptive to their ideas, desires, and interests. Our new partner falls off the pedestal not because we're suddenly seeing them realistically, but because we have gradually become less open to who they are. Things we easily accepted before, we now reject. *Our partner's fall from the pedestal is our own process of shutting down.*

Instead of seeing our partner through the nonjudging eyes of a new lover, we now see them through the beliefs we've developed about who they are and who they should be in relation to us. We think we're still seeing them objectively, but we're actually viewing them through the filter of our ever-increasing expectations. Then we wonder what happened to all the possibilities we sensed were there at the beginning.

If this sounds familiar, take heart. The more enlightened state you were in when you first met is all the proof you need that you have the ability to approach your relationship from a higher place.

WHAT ARE EXPECTATIONS?

When we're in a new relationship, we may feel we have finally found the perfect person to share our life with. In an effort to preserve our new-found happiness, we begin to form expectations to try to ensure that our partner continues to bring us everything we want or think we need.

This usually isn't a conscious process; it's simply part of what we've learned about how relationships work. Expectations, we're told, are unavoidable. We're not only conditioned to have them of our partner— we're even conditioned to expect our partner to have them of us.

Expectations are far more prevalent in our lives than we realize. Most of us bring an extensive collection to every new relationship, acquired from our families and friends, the media, and previous relationships. We add to them as our life with our partner takes new directions, like moving in together, buying a house, getting married, or starting a family.

Remember, expectations are beliefs about what someone should or should not do or how they should or should not behave. We have them about everyone in our lives, including ourselves. Here are just a few:

- "Karina should support my decisions."
- "Jonah shouldn't contradict me in public."

- "Paige should consult me before making plans with her friends."
- "Max shouldn't waste our money on lottery tickets."
- "Kristi shouldn't buy a latte every morning."
- "Ken should tell me when he's planning to do something that doesn't involve me."
- "Susie should want to have sex more often."
- "Kai should be more romantic."
- "I should be further along in my career."

Beneath these more obvious expectations is a layer of even subtler beliefs about how things should be. Underlying beliefs like these are so ingrained that they are often completely hidden from us:

- My partner should share my basic values and beliefs.
- My partner should understand me.
- My partner should know what I want.
- My partner should know how I feel.
- My partner should always be the same person I fell in love with.

"What about marriage?" you may be thinking. "We have to have expectations in marriage. That's one of the reasons we have marriage: so that we can depend on our partner to do certain things, and they can depend on us to do certain things in return." To an extent, this is true. If Phyllis's husband says he will pick up their daughter after school, Phyllis will certainly expect that he'll do his best to honor that agreement. If Walter's wife says she will make dinner that night, he naturally expects she will prepare enough for both of them.

What characterizes these agreements is the spirit in which they are made. Such agreements are entered into freely and mutually, without guilt or coercion. They are a natural component of cooperating together in the pursuit of a happy, satisfying life.

The expectations we're concerned with are those that don't stem from mutual agreement. They often involve an attempt to influence or control our partner. In one way or another, they will cause us to suffer when our partner doesn't meet them.

> Expectations strip away
> the potential for surprise,
> so the best
> they can produce
> is predictability.

It's impossible to overemphasize the damage expectations can do. Taken individually, some of our expectations may seem inconsequential or even acceptable. But a relationship can become so filled with them that, rather than being a source of joy, it begins to weigh us down. If we're not watchful, we might one day find ourselves trapped in a kind of "relationship hell."

HOW EXPECTATIONS
SHUT DOWN OUR RELATIONSHIPS

Any expectation we hold has the potential to produce disappointment, frustration, anger, and resentment. If you have an expectation and it's not met, how do you feel? Disappointed? Irritated? Angry? All of the above?

Expectations can also create indifference and even boredom. If you have an expectation and it *is* met, how do you feel? Thrilled? Overjoyed? Grateful? Probably not.

Though our expectations may give us a sense of security, we will never feel completely secure. On some level, we will always be anxious that one or more of them won't be met. On top of that, as Michael Naumer liked to point out, "Expectations shut down our partner's ability to bring us the very thing we want."

Suppose, for example, that it's very important to Kent to maintain a close sexual connection with his girlfriend. However, he knows from past experience that if Isabel looks at another man with interest, he'll feel jealous. To try to prevent that experience, he's done what many people do: He's formed an expectation that Isabel should not be physically attracted to anyone else.

Eventually, the inevitable happens. They're out together, having a great time, when Isabel catches sight of an attractive man across the room. Kent is instantly on guard, and things deteriorate quickly and predictably from there. He watches Isabel for signs of interest as he hears himself making an "innocent" comment with an obvious edge to it. Isabel feels the tension in the air and quickly figures out what the issue is. She then responds with some form of irritation of her own, like a sudden desire to leave or a curt "What's the matter?"

> With a minimum of expectations, a relationship is alive. It can breathe, grow, and expand.

No matter how Isabel reacts to Kent's jealousy, they are no longer connected—far from it. Unintentionally, he has shut down her ability to bring him what he really wants: a close sexual connection with her.

Similarly, take Eva, who has the expectation "Cory should want to spend Saturday evenings at home with me." Cory, however, prefers to play music with his buddies that night, as he always did before he met Eva. While it may be true that spending some Saturday nights together would be beneficial for their relationship, any action Eva takes based on her expectation will only put Cory on the defensive. Once he's feeling defensive, he will be even less receptive to anything she has to say.

As another example of how expectation can prevent us from having the experience we desire, consider Dan, whose partner, Jeanette, has been reluctant to initiate sex. He talks to her about it, communicating his desire for her to take a more active role once in a while. After that conversation, his expectation is that she will follow through, but night after night she doesn't. When Dan expresses his frustration to her, rather than giving him what he wants, it has the opposite effect: Jeanette becomes more uncomfortable, more self-conscious, and even less likely to initiate physical contact.

We'd all like our partner to continue to be interesting and exciting to us. But when they come up against our expectations about how they should act or behave, we practically ensure they won't be able to.

The best we can hope for when we have an expectation is that our partner

> No one likes to operate out of someone else's expectation.

will meet it. But it's human nature to respond to other people's expectations with resistance. Most of us don't like being told what to do. As that resistance builds, it will eventually suffocate the spontaneity and passion right out of our relationship.

IN THE ABSENCE OF EXPECTATION, EVERYTHING CAN BE A GIFT

Consider these two scenarios.

Cheryl and Kevin have been dating almost a year. It's Friday night. Cheryl has an expectation she and Kevin will see each other tonight, as they often spend weekend evenings together. When Kevin calls to ask her out, she says yes, but feels no real excitement about their upcoming date. "This relationship seems to be losing its passion," she tells herself.

Abby and Geoff have also been dating almost a year. It's Friday night, and although she and Geoff often spend weekend evenings together, Abby has no expectation they will do so tonight. She's open to whatever the evening might bring, even if it's not her boyfriend. When the phone rings and it's Geoff, she's excited about getting together with him.

Abby knows that having expectations in her relationship won't increase the love or happiness she experiences. It's not that she never has expectations. But she's discovered that the fewer she has, the more connected and alive her relationship is. So she makes it a point to watch for and let go of her expectations whenever she can. Geoff, without the burden of expectation on him, feels a sense of freedom in the relationship, and that's exciting to him.

The more beliefs you have about who your partner should be and what they should do, the less you will truly see them and the more you will limit their ability to surprise you. *In the absence of expectation, every encounter and interaction you have can be a gift.*

What gift can your partner offer you if all they do is meet your expectations?

RECOGNIZE YOUR EXPECTATIONS

Therapists often recommend that couples identify and then share their expectations with one another. Partners are told they can improve their chances of living up to each other's expectations if they communicate their expectations clearly and then work to adjust their attitudes, behaviors, and goals to accommodate them as much as possible.

Some therapists go a step further and suggest that couples honestly evaluate their expectations to see whether they are realistic. The key to a successful relationship, they say, is having realistic expectations of the relationship and each other.

These suggestions may be steps in the right direction, but they overlook a very important fact: *Expectations are simply beliefs. Like all beliefs, expectations can be changed or even eliminated.*

Remember that every expectation that isn't the result of a simple mutual agreement has the potential to create disappointment, frustration, anger, and resentment. So a powerful way to experience more joy in your relationship is to recognize your expectations and then reduce their influence or, ideally, eliminate them altogether.

If you're thinking this will require focus and determination, you're absolutely right. But when you understand that your expectations are essentially choices you're making about how to relate to others, simply being aware of them will begin to lessen their impact. It's unlikely that many of us will rid ourselves of all our expectations, but the more we reduce or eliminate them, the more relationship satisfaction we will experience.

Accusations

Accusations are one of the most obvious signs of an expectation. "Why didn't you bring any money?" "You said you'd be ready on time." The words "never" and "always" are instant giveaways: "You never give me credit for what I contribute." "You always want to do the same old thing."

We often try to disguise our accusations by choosing words that don't sound accusatory. But our tone of voice and the words we emphasize give us away every time. For example, imagine how a man who is *curious* about his girlfriend's evening would ask this question: "What did you do last night?" Now imagine how a man who is *suspicious* about his girlfriend's evening would ask the same question.

> **Any statement made in an accusatory tone of voice signals an underlying expectation.**

If there's even a hint of accusation behind any statement you make or question you ask, your partner will know it immediately. You will know it, too. If your partner suggests that you've made some kind of an accusation (and especially if you hear yourself responding defensively, "All I said was . . ."), take an honest look at yourself to see if that's the case.

"You Should," "You Know," "You Remember"

If there's one word that is almost always a sign of an expectation, it's "should." It's hard to use the word without implying that something needs to be done differently for you to be satisfied. Unless you're offering directions or making simple recommendations ("You should turn right at the bank to avoid the construction." "You should take your umbrella because it's probably going to rain."), using "should" with another person almost certainly implies that he or she is not doing something right.

The phrases "you know" and "you remember" are also likely indicators of an expectation. We frequently use them to imply that our significant other should remember everything we've told them and all we've experienced together: "You know I don't like eating dinner so late." "You were there—you know as well as I do." "Don't you remember that my father's visiting that week?"

We often assume our memories all work the same way, but the truth is, some people recall dates and numbers with ease, while others find it difficult to remember the birthdays of their closest friends. Some recall events in detail, while others barely remember that they attended.

Heather has been focusing on letting go of her belief that her husband's memory should work like hers. She says, "Now when I hear the words coming out of my mouth—something like, 'You remember, I told you about it last week'—I stop, take a breath, and start over."

In addition to having memories that operate differently, we also have unique ways of processing experiences. It's unrealistic to expect that other people will respond to the world in the same way we do— that what bothers us will bother them and that what's important to us will be important to them.

Fixing Your Partner in Place

People who have been together awhile may one day find themselves saying, "It's become so predictable. There's no excitement any more; we just know each other too well." Michael Naumer talked about how easily relationships grow stagnant when we "fix" our partner, meaning fix them in place by forming a set of beliefs about them and thinking we now "know" who they are.

> To truly see someone means to see them without preconceptions.

We begin to develop ideas about who our partner is right from the start. The problem is, *we then make assumptions about how they will be or will act in the future.* Consider these statements:

- "I can't get Julian to go dancing. I've tried."

- "Lauren doesn't like to talk about feelings."

- "Chris simply isn't willing to try anything new."

Couples often reinforce this habit with one another:

- "Why did you order this? You know I don't like seafood."

- "I don't want to go on a cruise ship. You know I'm uncomfortable around strangers."

When our partner does or says something that conflicts with our assumptions, we often react with fear, resistance, or disbelief: "Why do you want to go in there? You don't even like art!"

Think about the ways you may be fixing your partner. Can you identify any limiting ideas you have about how he or she should act or behave?

Emotional Indicators

Watching your emotions can also help you uncover your expectations. Whenever you experience a separating emotion—such as frustration, disappointment, irritation, blame, or anger—it probably points to an idea you have that the world or someone in it should be doing something differently.

If we feel frustrated when our partner doesn't check with us before making plans to do something with his or her friends, or jealous when they call an ex-lover to wish them happy birthday, we might look to see if there's an expectation at work.

> Every time you feel resentful or disappointed, ask yourself, *What expectation am I holding?*

Suppose Victoria becomes irritated when she discovers that her husband didn't put gas in the car. That the gas tank didn't get filled is just "what is." What's making her irritated is her unmet expectation that her husband should have remembered to fill it.

What's essential to recognize is that Victoria's expectation doesn't change reality one bit: The tank is empty either way. It does, though, have a significantly negative effect on the connection she feels with her husband.

DON'T ACT OUT OF YOUR EXPECTATION

Once you recognize that you have an expectation, you have the opportunity to immediately reduce its negative impact by simply *doing nothing*.

When you're upset, your actions tend to be unconscious *reactions*. Speaking with an edge to your voice, making accusations, using sarcasm, and withdrawing are all typical responses to unmet expectations. Such reactions will likely be met by counter-reactions from your partner. Think about this: When someone comes at you with an accusation or addresses you in a sarcastic tone of voice, how do you

> You lose the possibility of connecting with your partner when you're under the influence of an expectation.

respond? Unless you're one of the enlightened few, you strike back in some way, even if only through quiet withdrawal.

If possible, *resist the temptation to let your expectation direct your words or actions*. It only takes one small comment to trigger an exchange of defensive or accusatory statements that can quickly spiral out of control.

Note that withdrawing is not the same as doing nothing. When we withdraw, we purposely keep ourselves removed from the shared emotional space, refusing to reenter it. When we do nothing, we remain open to re-engaging with our partner.

Teaching yourself not to act when you're being influenced by an expectation is challenging. Most of us have spent a lifetime trying to control people and circumstances through our expectations. At first you may not even recognize that you're acting out of an expectation until long after the moment has passed. With practice, the time between the appearance of an expectation and your recognition that it has control of you will lessen. One day you will find yourself watching your emerging expectations before they have the chance to influence what you do or say.

EVALUATE YOUR EXPECTATION

Once you've created some space between you and your expectation, consider how well it has worked for you in the past. Has it made you feel more connected and improved your relationship? Or has it caused disagreements and arguments and made you feel anxious, disappointed, or disillusioned? *How much satisfaction has it really brought you?*

David recognized he had an expectation that his girlfriend shouldn't interrupt him. At first his mind tried to justify his belief. "People shouldn't interrupt. It's inconsiderate." Once he was able to look beyond these justifications and honestly evaluate how well his expectation had worked for him, he saw that it had only made him frustrated and angry. In addition, whenever he'd expressed his belief to his girlfriend, it started an argument that left them both feeling unheard, defensive, and resentful.

It takes courage to be honest with yourself about how your expectations have influenced your behavior.

Renée had been operating for years under this expectation: "Rob shouldn't be attracted to other women." When she took an honest look at how this had played out in her relationship, she saw that she became uncomfortable and suspicious almost any time an attractive woman was nearby.

"I've sometimes questioned Rob about his actions and intentions, which makes him defensive," she admits. "There have even been times I've manipulated things to keep him away from certain women."

Renée recognized that her attempts to control Rob always left her feeling embarrassed and insecure.

Once you've analyzed what an expectation has done for you, consider this question: *If you continue to have this expectation, how likely is it to bring you satisfaction in the future?*

DISCOVER THE DESIRE
BENEATH YOUR EXPECTATION

Once you've identified an expectation and understand that it is unlikely to get you what you want, you're ready to try a much more effective approach. The secret to this approach lies in knowing that beneath every expectation (sometimes far beneath) is a natural, authentic desire to connect with those you love. *Coming from this authentic desire is an opportunity to experience true connection in your relationship.*

At first you may question the idea that there's an authentic desire beneath every expectation. But consider that, at their very heart, relationships exist because of our natural longing for human connection. Once we've experienced the feeling of true connection with someone, most of us begin to fear we will lose it. We then develop expectations to try to "hold it all in place."

You must strip away your expectation and look below the surface to discover the authentic desire underneath. Ask yourself, *What am I trying to get from this expectation? What am I really after?* Then try to capture your authentic desire in a concise statement.

If you find yourself insisting, "My authentic desire is for my girlfriend to give me her full attention when I speak" or "What I really want is for my partner not to be attracted to anyone else," you haven't gone deep enough. *If your statement seeks to manipulate or control your partner in any way, you are still dealing with an expectation.*

It may take considerable investigation to discover your authentic desire. When Renée evaluated her expectation "Rob shouldn't be attracted to other women," her mind at first only produced variations of it: "Rob should only be attracted to me." "We should only be attracted to each other." She also found herself justifying her belief: "Rob and I promised to be monogamous. That means we should only show interest toward each other. Everyone would agree with that."

Notice that every one of these statements is still a subtle attempt to exert control. *An authentic desire never seeks to restrict, inhibit, or restrain another person in any way. An authentic desire has no "should" quality to it.*

When Renée was finally able to state her desire in a way that was free from manipulation and control, it looked like this: "What I really want, deep down, is to feel sexually connected to Rob all the time."

Similarly, David, who became frustrated whenever he felt interrupted by his girlfriend, stated his authentic desire as "I want to feel really connected when we communicate."

Like every authentic desire, both of these statements say nothing about what someone else should or shouldn't do. They do not try to alter or restrict another person's behavior in any way. They are expressions of love rather than of fear. When your statement meets these criteria, you have found your authentic desire.

EXPRESS YOUR DESIRE
AS AN INVITATION

The beauty of uncovering your authentic desire is that *you can turn any desire into an invitation*. And a simple, heartfelt invitation can open the door for a truly rewarding experience.

Maria, a landscape architect, recognized that she had been relating to her husband through this expectation: "Jonathon should want to go dancing with me because I enjoy it so much." For years she complained about Jonathon not accompanying her, which only made him less interested.

When Maria examined her expectation, she eventually arrived at this authentic desire: "I'd like to share my passion for dancing with

161

the man I love." Notice that this statement expresses a desire for connection with Jonathon and doesn't seek to control him in any way.

By coming from her authentic desire, Maria could now *invite* her husband to experience her love of dance with her, even if he never sets foot on a dance floor. "I know you've never had much interest in dancing," she might say to him, "but I'd love to take you to a club anyway. We could just hang out and watch the people dance, and I could tell you what I love about it."

An expectation can be met in only one way. An authentic desire can be fulfilled in as many ways as you can dream of.

Be aware that if you offer your partner an invitation, they may be reluctant or even say no. If their refusal irritates you, this is a sign you're still holding some expectation about it. Remind yourself that *a true invitation is free of obligation*. The person you're inviting has the freedom to accept or decline—without pressure, judgment, or repercussions.

Let's look back at Renée, who identified her authentic desire as "What I really want is to feel sexually connected to Rob all the time." The next time they're out together, she might get the courage to whisper to him, "I'd really love to know what you find attractive. How would you feel about showing me?"

To be successful at this, Renée has to approach Rob differently than she has in the past. It's imperative that she create a safe space in which he can honestly express whatever feelings or thoughts he has. It's also essential that she come from a place of love and acceptance rather than fear. This can be challenging, especially if she's been operating for years from an expectation that Rob shouldn't have been looking in the first place.

To come from a place of love, stay focused on your authentic desire. If Renée wants to experience a special, sexy connection with Rob, she has to allow him the freedom to experience himself as a sexy person, even if that means his attention is occasionally directed somewhere other than toward her. Remember, *it's vital to present your invitations in a loving, accepting way and to be open to however your partner responds.* This is not about manipulating others into doing things they don't want to do. It's about inviting them to take another look and see something they didn't see before.

Getting your expectations met is not nearly as much fun as having your invitations accepted!

David, who identified his authentic desire as "I want to feel really connected when we communicate," might research workshops that explore ways for couples to communicate more lovingly. Then he might say to his girlfriend, "You know that I've gotten frustrated when I think you're interrupting me. Well, I don't want to do that anymore. So I'm wondering if you'd be interested in taking this workshop with me." With this invitation, David isn't putting any blame on his girlfriend. If she isn't interested, he can always go to a workshop on his own. Even if only one person makes a positive change in how he or she communicates, the couple's entire dynamic is likely to shift for the better.

Can you imagine if instead of getting upset with your husband for forgetting your anniversary, you simply invited him to celebrate it with you? Or when you've told him you love roses, yet he's never brought you any, you pick some up yourself and invite him to enjoy them with you?

It takes willingness and bravery to approach your partner in a new way, especially if you've been operating out of expectation for a long time. Be assured that as you practice uncovering the authentic desires beneath your expectations and turning those desires into invitations, the process will become easier. While an invitation is no guarantee of your partner's participation, you will be making a positive shift in how you approach the relationship.

Of course, your partner is likely to have as many expectations about you as you have about him or her. Most of us understand that we can't force our significant other to change. However, we can be a powerful example. As we reduce or eliminate our expectations, our partner will feel the reduction in "should" energy directed their way. More importantly, they're bound to notice that we're becoming much happier and may be very curious to know what we've been up to!

When you learn to relate through invitation rather than expectation,
you'll be getting a lot more "yeses" from your partner.
In time, you will be able to identify and address new expectations
as they arise. By continuing to free yourself from expectations,
your relationship will be rewarded with more of the
sparkle and excitement that was so abundant early on.

9

Transforming the Energy of Jealousy

The energy of jealousy may be our greatest untapped resource
for infusing our relationships with passion and excitement.
When you learn how to approach and channel that energy
through love instead of through fear, jealousy
has the potential to contribute to your relationship
in ways you may never have imagined.

J ealousy. The word alone makes a lot of people squirm. We don't like to admit we're feeling jealous, we don't enjoy how we feel and act when we are, and most of us don't have effective ways of handling it. Jealousy can overtake us in an instant and leave us feeling embarrassed, angry, and out of control. We can find ourselves consumed with fear, imagining the worst, rehearsing what we'll say—or even plotting our revenge.

Jealousy can surface in any relationship, including in platonic friendships and between family members, but it isn't an issue for everyone. Some people have had relatively little experience with it, while others struggle with it constantly. Some people feel uncomfortable whenever their partner shows interest in somebody else, even if it's only someone in a movie or a magazine. Then there are those for whom jealousy is much less frequent. It comes up only when they discover that their partner has been holding back details about a particular friendship or is actually seeing someone else. In most relationships where jealousy is an issue, one person is considerably more affected by it than the other, making things feel out of balance.

Sometimes the signs of jealousy are obvious. Ryan recalls being very jealous in college. Whenever he saw his girlfriend in conversation with another man, he would press her for details later. "So what were you two talking about? Does he live around here? Where does he work?" Sierra, who's in her early twenties, says that when she notices her boyfriend looking at another woman, she gives him a friendly punch on the arm and announces, "Hey, I'm over here!"

Other people are more indirect. "If Marco looks at someone else," Michelle says, "I just get quiet and try to let him know that his behavior isn't okay with me."

Many people say a little jealousy is a good thing, as it indicates our partner's desire for us and shows they care. Some believe that jealousy is useful for keeping a partner from straying. But rather than creating a loving environment in which a relationship can truly thrive, the ways we typically handle jealousy discourage, and may even prevent, real connection.

The ideas in this chapter might sound radical, as they're very different from how most people approach jealousy. But if you or your partner suffers from this powerful emotion, these ideas might help transform your experience of jealousy from one of *disconnection* into one of *increased connection*.

It's important to recognize here that the great majority of situations where jealousy is a factor involve only a perceived threat to a relationship, not a real one. Most people in monogamous relationships don't *want* to have affairs. What they do want is a close, exciting, connected experience with another human being (*you*, if possible!). However, if you happen to be facing a situation in which your partner really is involved with someone else, be sure to read "What If the Threat Is Real?" later in this chapter. If your relationship has the potential for violence or abuse around jealousy or any other issue, it's vital to take care of yourself by seeking support as soon as possible. There are always family members, friends, counselors, crisis centers, or hotlines that will help you get perspective on your situation and decide on the best course of action.

WHY JEALOUSY SHOWS UP

This may come as a surprise, but we don't experience jealousy because our partner finds someone else interesting or attractive. *We experience jealousy because of what we tell ourselves about our partner finding someone else interesting or attractive.* If you've rarely or never felt jealous, this means you don't torture yourself with the kinds of thoughts that produce this emotion.

Jealousy is often a response to the fear that our partner will be sexually active outside of our relationship: "He probably thinks she's younger and cuter than I am. Is she interested in him?" Feelings of jealousy are also caused by worries that our partner will form an emotional attachment to someone else: "She shouldn't be spending so much time talking to him. She should be over here with me."

Comparisons, and thoughts of inadequacy or inferiority, may bring on immediate feelings of jealousy: "She's more talented and more entertaining than I am." "I just know I don't satisfy her." "He's more interested in her because she's in such good shape." We may believe that if our partner pays attention to someone else, it means we're not the most special in his or her eyes.

Fears that our significant other might lose interest in us or betray us may also bring about an attack of the green monster: "If he gets to know her, he'll wish he wasn't in a committed relationship with me." "She's bound to meet someone more confident and successful if she goes to that motivational seminar."

> The thought "He thinks she's prettier than I am" can turn a romantic evening into a miserable one.

As you might recall from Chapter 1, our minds will dutifully go out in search of evidence to support our beliefs. Fueled by jealousy, we can usually find plenty of it. In this vicious cycle, the more evidence we collect, the more real we believe the threat is.

Society justifies and reinforces our jealous reactions. Long before we've even experienced our first crush, we've learned from family, friends, and the media that if our boyfriend or girlfriend shows interest in someone else, we have every right to be jealous. We get the message loud and clear that we simply *will* experience jealousy if the person we're with looks at someone else with appreciation or desire. Once we're old enough to date, it would be surprising if we *didn't* react with jealousy in such circumstances.

If you struggle with feelings of jealousy or if your partner experiences them, know that these feelings are quite normal. Some experts think they may even be an evolutionary instinct. By trying to make certain that her man (her family's meat provider) wasn't led astray by the attractive female in the next cave, a woman might help to ensure her children's survival. Similarly, a man wouldn't want the meat he's hunted going to support genes that aren't his.

Evolutionary or not, *we have been conditioned to believe that love and affection are limited*. Even if our partner's attention is only momentarily directed toward someone else, many of us interpret that as a loss of interest in us. Naomi puts it quite simply: "If my boyfriend gives another woman attention, there'll be less love for me." Naomi might be surprised to discover that if her boyfriend doesn't feel he has to give her all his attention when they're out together, the attention he does give her will be much more authentic and heartfelt.

WHY ACTIONS TAKEN OUT OF JEALOUSY
WON'T BRING US CLOSER TOGETHER

Jealousy itself is not the problem. It's our typical *approaches* to it that can limit a couple's ability to feel close and connected. Any actions we take out of jealousy are unlikely to bring about the love and security we're after. They won't diminish our partner's natural attraction to other people, and they won't increase our partner's desire for us.

Controlling Our Partner's Behavior

The majority of us, often subconsciously, enter a relationship with a mental list of what our partner is committing to at the moment we agree to be exclusive. One common expectation is that our partner should only be attracted to us. Though the agreements related to this belief vary (and are often unspoken), they generally look something like this: We won't take too much notice of other people when we're out together, we won't hug or make eye contact for too long, we won't have close friends of a particular gender, and we won't text, email, or call people who might be seen as a threat.

When we're really in love with someone, our attraction to others does tend to lessen significantly. And some people really do only have eyes for each other. But the majority of us don't suddenly cease being attracted to other people the moment we commit to a monogamous relationship.

> **The belief that our partner should only be attracted to us reduces our chances of having a truly connected relationship.**

If we find that our partner isn't living up to our ideas about how they should behave, we may attempt to curb their natural attraction to other people. We might indirectly let them know that we don't appreciate their behavior: "You sure like the waitresses here, don't you?" Or we might outright accuse them of not being committed. We might show them how hurt or disappointed we feel if they buy a racy magazine or look at erotica online. Or we might make comments like the one Virginia heard from her husband one afternoon: "Did you put that lipstick on before or after you met with the real estate agent?"

Thinking that the only way to alleviate our jealousy is to get control of the situation, we may try to establish rules about what our partner should or shouldn't do: "I'd prefer it if you didn't kiss your women friends hello." "I think you should dress more conservatively when you're out with your girlfriends." "You shouldn't let your guy friends give you a ride home."

> If you keep your partner in captivity, they'll always be wondering what's outside the cage.

If our partner complies with requests like these, it may give us a temporary sense of relief from our jealous feelings. But their compliance won't address the real cause of our jealousy. As we try to rein in our partner by controlling their behavior and making them feel guilty for their natural attractions, they may feel like a noose is slowly being tightened around them. It's easy to understand why resentment can soon build up.

Many people respond to the restrictions placed on them by pulling away from their partner, which is the opposite of what we really want. As Justin says, "You don't look at other women while your wife is looking at *you*, so you really can't be yourself when you're with her."

Christopher agrees. "A guy's typical response to his girlfriend's jealousy is to go underground. We're still looking, but we're always worried we're going to get busted. So we try to make sure we're not noticed doing something we're not 'supposed' to be doing."

Interrogating and Attacking

When we allow our jealous feelings to control our behavior, we may find ourselves interrogating or attacking our partner. Our need for reassurance may lead us to question their thoughts, intentions, or actions.

Richard, an attorney, says that when he's afraid his girlfriend has her eye on someone else, he makes comments like "You didn't give me much attention at the party. I'm upset that you spent so much time talking to Miles." Richard is making an effort to express his feelings, which is a positive step. But notice that he is still putting the responsibility for his feelings on his girlfriend.

Some accusations are more direct: "Where did you go after work? Who did you see there? Are you attracted to her?" Questions like these will immediately put our partner on the defensive. They may start to worry about whether they have their story straight—even when they don't have a story! They may get nervous or become cautious about how much they reveal. We might then interpret their reactions as signs that our suspicions are warranted.

Doug, a carpenter, puts it this way: "When my wife starts giving me the third degree about where I've been and who I saw, I instantly wonder if there's anything that's not okay to say. I always feel like I'm just one step away from a wrong answer."

Avoiding Triggering Situations

Some people attempt to steer their partner clear of situations that might bring out their own jealousy. They might try to avoid going to parties, dance clubs, or movies with a sexy theme.

Mia, a hair stylist, frequently changes her plans for exactly this reason. When she and her boyfriend are invited to an event where she thinks she might have competition for his attention, she will "act disinterested and try to get him to do something else." She also tries to make sure he doesn't attend social functions without her. She once accepted an invitation to see a movie with a friend. When she learned that her boyfriend's office was having a get-together that same evening, she canceled her plans so he wouldn't have an opportunity to socialize with the women in his office. Mia is embarrassed about these manipulative behaviors, and they probably leave her boyfriend mystified.

Lauri, a ballroom dancer, says jealousy on the dance floor is common "because you're constantly in the arms of other men and women. You go thinking you're going to have a good time, and then the little green monster ruins your evening." Because of this, she says, "Couples often drop out of the dance world."

If you're always trying to get out of situations you might find uncomfortable, you won't be able to maintain a strong, intimate connection with your partner. You'll also be missing out on opportunities to approach jealousy in ways that will actually *strengthen* the bond between you.

Denying or Withdrawing

Some of us try to deny or cover up our feelings of jealousy. Amanda, a graduate student, says, "On the outside, I pretend to be cool with it. I'm sure Jamie doesn't know how hurt I feel about his close friendships with other women. And I know they're just friends, so my feelings don't even make sense. I'd rather he didn't even know about them."

Stacey, an accountant, believes that if she were more evolved, she would be fine with pretty much anything her partner, Jen, wanted to do. So when jealousy strikes, Stacey keeps her discomfort to herself in an attempt to prevent her mood from affecting her partner. Jen, feeling the distance between them, doesn't know what's wrong or how to reconnect with Stacey.

When we withdraw from our partner with the belief that we're giving them space to be themselves, the freedom we're offering is a false freedom—purchased at the expense of our connection. Acknowledging and accepting our jealous feelings is the first step along the path toward *true* freedom from jealousy. This includes acknowledging and letting go of any anger or embarrassment we have accumulated from jealousy we've experienced in the past. If you've denied or ignored these emotions in yourself, turn back to "Into Me I See" in Chapter 3 for a reminder on how to release them.

THE ALLURE OF THE FORBIDDEN FRUIT

Keeping your partner on a leash doesn't only breed resentment. The more control you try to exert, the more your partner is likely to be drawn to things that don't involve you. Brad experienced this with his first wife. "When we'd go out, I wasn't supposed to make any more conversation with the waitress—let alone eye contact—than was necessary to order dinner. But I'm a friendly guy! Sure, she might be attractive,

When we feel we're living life on restriction, we quickly become resentful of the one making the rules.

but I also really like to talk with people. My wife would give me the evil eye when she'd decided I'd been talking to the waitress too long. After a while, it was just easier to go to dinner without her."

It's also possible that if you make your partner's natural attractions off limits, his or her desire may actually intensify. It's human nature to want what we're told we can't have. As Marcelo explains, "When women question a guy and try to control his every move, it actually makes it more likely his attention will be drawn somewhere else."

Brigitte, a college student, agrees. "If a guy's jealous of me for no reason, it pushes me in that direction, since I've already been made out to be a bad girl."

If trying to keep your partner from being attracted to other people won't strengthen your connection, what will? Believe it or not, what *will* help is accepting that it's natural to have attractions to other people, even in a committed relationship. If you restrict your partner, the pull to experience those attractions will continue to build—and in a way that will be separate from you. Imagine what might happen if the object of your partner's attraction welcomes his or her attention while you approach your partner with suspicion or anger. *If you create a receptive, loving space that expands to include your natural attractions as part of your relationship, the desire to act on them will lessen or even dissolve.*

Just ask Tony, who works at a popular wine bar. "I talk and even flirt with all kinds of women every day. It's one of the reasons my side of the bar is always busy! My previous girlfriends have all been bugged by that. I can tell you that when my attraction to someone else is taboo, I'm thinking about her all the time. The girlfriend I have now is comfortable with the fact that I happen to be a flirt, so I hardly ever think about other women. And all my friends think she's cool as hell!"

Vanessa, an accountant, feels the same way. "Because my boyfriend is fine with my flirtatious nature, I have no desire to go out and make something happen with someone else."

It's understandable if this approach to a committed relationship makes you nervous. If you've been in a partnership in which being attracted to other people is off limits, it may be hard to imagine what Tony and Vanessa are talking about. Contemplating being in a relationship without the usual controls in place can be scary. But those controls, and the predictability they produce, may unintentionally lead to complacency, boredom, resentment, or even affairs. By consciously experimenting with relaxing those controls, it's actually possible to *increase* the passion and connection in a loving, committed relationship.

It's important to be clear about the kind of flirting Vanessa and Tony are referring to. This is not about engaging

If you and your partner are experimenting with a little healthy flirtation, always be aware of the *spirit* in which you're flirting.

with another person in an attempt to start a romantic or sexual relationship with them. It's certainly not about flirting with the intention of "getting back" at your partner for something you feel they did. This is innocent flirtation: interacting in a healthy, playful way with no purpose beyond feeling attractive and attracted. Rather than flirting in an attempt to make up for a *lack* of connection you're feeling with your partner, you're flirting in a spirit of *full* connection with them.

WHAT TO DO
WHEN JEALOUSY SHOWS UP

The pain of jealousy can be all-consuming. When we're feeling this pain, all we want is immediate relief. True relief, however, doesn't come from trying to control what's going on *out there*. Instead, the answer lies in transforming what's going on *in here*, in our own experience.

Michael Naumer often said, "Don't assign responsibility for your emotional experience to your partner." The wisdom in these words is clear when we look at the emotion of jealousy. When we're in the middle of a jealous reaction, most of us have a tendency to blame our partner. In one way or another, we communicate this message: "You have to stop doing what you're doing, because I'm being hurt by it."

The first step to freeing ourselves from the pain of this emotion is to remind ourselves that jealousy is normal and to treat ourselves with compassion.

"By giving myself permission to feel what I'm feeling," Lauri explains, "I'm instantly relaxed around the whole issue. The jealousy is no longer in control."

The second step is to take responsibility for our jealousy. We do this by recognizing that *our beliefs and the thoughts they generate—not our partner's behavior—are the cause of our experience.* Taking on this responsibility, of course, can be difficult to do. It's human nature to assume that

> When you're
> feeling jealous,
> don't make it worse
> by being
> hard on yourself.
> Show some compassion!

the person we're experiencing jealousy over is the person who can easily end it. But when we decide to take responsibility for our own feelings, we gain the personal power we need to create a positive experience for ourselves. We no longer have to wait for and hope that someone else will do it for us.

If you're used to manipulating people and situations in an attempt to alleviate your jealousy, be assured that it really is possible to train yourself not to let those powerful feelings direct your words or actions. Remember, any control you might be able to exert over your partner won't bring you closer together. The only thing it's sure to produce is frustration and resentment.

Taking action to reduce your jealousy doesn't mean you're giving other people permission to take advantage of you. On the contrary, *the number one reason to reduce your own jealousy is to create a better experience for yourself.*

In addition to not allowing your feelings to direct your behavior, do your best not to continue feeding a jealous reaction with your thoughts. Obsessive thinking is unproductive and will only add to your discomfort. Additionally, try not to judge or criticize yourself ("I shouldn't be reacting this way; this isn't who I want to be"). Acknowledge and accept what you're experiencing. This takes practice. But if you stay with it and don't fuel your reaction with more negative thinking, your feelings of jealousy will eventually begin to lessen. At that point, you'll be able to take a look at the thoughts that generated them.

Distinguish Envy from Jealousy

When you're experiencing a jealous reaction, it can be helpful to determine whether part of your reaction is actually envy.

- Envy is the desire to have something *someone else* has.

- Jealousy is the fear of losing something *you* have (or think you have).

If you find that part of your reaction is based in envy, you can use it as a source of inspiration to draw what you desire into your life.

Melissa, a clothes designer, says, "If I meet somebody who has a beautiful house, I think, 'Oh, that means I could have one too, since someone I know has one.' This way I channel my feelings into something constructive and positive."

How might this play out in a relationship? For years, Nick regularly got upset when his wife went out dancing with her girlfriends. His wife was frustrated with his reaction to something she considered harmless. When Nick finally took a look at what was behind his reaction, he concluded that it wasn't a fear of losing his wife's attention or love, but a desire to have a similar experience himself. He realized that he missed getting together with friends like he did when he was single.

> Envy can inspire you to move in the direction of something you desire.

"I'm much happier now that I occasionally make time to see a movie or play pool with a buddy. I'm comfortable with Leslie going out too, because I see what she gets from it."

With Nick's blessing to enjoy her evenings out, Leslie says she's happier as well.

Transform Your Jealousy-Creating Beliefs

Once you've found the inspiration in the envy part of your reaction, if there is one, you can turn to the jealousy part. Identify the beliefs that are causing your feelings, and then find replacement beliefs for them. If you haven't been practicing this technique, you may want to revisit Chapter 1.

Remind yourself of the connection between what you think ("He's noticed that woman over there; now I'll get less of his attention") and how you subsequently feel (anxious, undesirable, or even angry). Then do your best to identify the specific thoughts that are responsible for your reaction. These thoughts are sometimes so far in the background that they can be difficult to pinpoint. But if the emotion arises, the thoughts are sure to be there somewhere.

Once you've listed the thoughts behind your reaction, put into words the belief responsible for producing them. Since jealousy often goes to the very heart of our self-esteem issues, it may well turn out to be a core belief like "I'm unlovable," "I'm unattractive," or "There isn't enough love for me."

When you have a clear statement of your belief, come up with a replacement belief that will be available to you the next time you're in a similar situation. It might be something like "Alexis shows me how much she loves me in so many ways" or "I feel attractive because I take care of myself." Remind yourself of your new belief often enough that it will be there when you need it.

Karen has years of experience with jealousy. "It used to be that every time I was out with my husband and a pretty woman was nearby," she says, "I became completely paralyzed."

When she decided to investigate her reaction, Karen realized that part of it was really based in envy. "The minute I entered a room, I would scan all the women there and pick out anything that I felt put me at a disadvantage: She's younger, she's more athletic, she's more talented, her outfit is sexier."

Karen has now learned to channel these types of comparisons into inspiration. "Now when I have these thoughts, I think to myself, 'I'd like to try that with *my* hair' or 'Look how fit she is; I'm going to sign up for that spin class' or 'I wonder how I'd look in that dress? I think I'll ask where she got it.'"

Once she'd separated out the envy part of her reaction, Karen examined the other self-defeating thoughts she has in these situations, like "I'm not as intellectual as these people" or "This skirt doesn't look that good on me." She phrased the belief behind them as "I'll never be attractive enough." This belief, she could see, was based on an impossible standard—one she held for herself and apparently no one else. Through this realization, she learned the importance of putting her attention on what was unique and beautiful about herself rather than on her perceived inadequacies. For her replacement belief, she chose "I'm attractive just the way I am."

"Now before I go out, I find something to focus on that evening, like my smile or my sense of humor," she says. "If negative thoughts start to come up, I go back to the positive one I brought with me."

What If the Threat Is Real?

Most jealousy situations involve only a perceived threat to a relationship, not a real one. But what if your partner behaves in a way that the majority of people would feel is inappropriate, such as passionately kissing someone else? Or what if your partner comes home and tells you he or she is having an affair?

In these situations, you'll likely experience a range of intense emotions, jealousy being just one. Do your best not to continually feed these emotions with thoughts like "How could she have done this to me after all we've been through? Don't I matter to her? She said she loved me!" Be aware of such thoughts, but try not to follow or hold onto them. This can be challenging, but it's infinitely more effective than allowing your emotions to spiral out of control. Remember, it's these thoughts that are producing much of the emotional pain you're experiencing.

At the same time, remember not to ignore or suppress the

painful feelings you are experiencing. Turn back to "Into Me I See" in Chapter 3, which describes a process for acknowledging and releasing emotions. In this practice, you might remember, the intention is to process and release your emotions by fully feeling their effects in your body without adding to them with more negative thinking.

Before you make any decisions about how to move forward, you might want to talk the situation over with a trusted friend or counselor. *Whatever approach you take to the situation, do your best not to respond or make decisions out of feelings like anger, betrayal, or despair.* Actions fueled by these emotions won't be infused with either wisdom or love.

It can be especially challenging at these times to remember your relationship context (see Chapter 6) and the idea that everything has the potential to contribute to your life in some way. But it's more important now than ever, as this is the most direct way to get back to a connected experience with your partner, if that's what you want. Whatever the eventual outcome, finding your way through this transition will be easier if you allow yourself the necessary time to make any decisions from a place of awareness, acceptance, and love. This is true even if the situation leads to you and your partner separating or otherwise changing the degree to which you're involved in each other's lives.

What If Your Partner Experiences Jealousy?

If your significant other experiences jealousy and understands that their jealousy is their own responsibility, the most supportive thing you can do is to provide a safe, loving space for them to examine their reaction and get to the heart of what's causing it. You might offer to stay with them while they do so. If any accusations arise, simply notice them and let them go by; do your best not to respond defensively. If it feels right, you might assist your partner with this process by asking questions like "What are you experiencing? What are you telling yourself that brings on these emotions?" Most importantly, let your partner know that you love them and believe they are capable of finding their way through this.

If your partner points to you as the cause of their jealousy, just your knowing that their feelings are really their responsibility will begin to alter the dynamic between you. When you stop modifying your behavior in order to minimize their reactions, your relationship will begin to shift. You may even want to be open with them about what you're doing and why. Reassure them that you love them and understand that they feel uncomfortable about certain things you do, but explain that you no longer want to take responsibility for their feelings.

If your partner doesn't seem inclined to take responsibility for their jealousy, see "What If My Partner Isn't Interested in Reducing *Their* Baggage?" in Chapter 3. This section describes the three choices available to you if your partner doesn't have an interest in doing what's necessary to create a truly connected experience.

Of course, this is all assuming that your partner's jealousy is in response to a *perceived* threat to your relationship, not a real one. If your actions are posing a genuine threat, you've got some soul searching to do. It might take some effort to step back from your relationship and raise your awareness of what you're doing. You might want to reflect on questions like these: *Is this the relationship I want to be in right now? If it is, what kind of person do I want to be in it?*

Finally, if your relationship has the potential for violence or abuse around jealousy or any other issue, make it a priority to find professional help or other support. You might also decide to change your level of involvement in the relationship or even get out of it altogether. If so, use the opportunity to do the personal exploration necessary to raise your own sense of self-worth and avoid attracting this dynamic into your life again.

TRANSFORMING JEALOUSY
INTO APPRECIATION

We can only fully appreciate the gift of having someone in our lives when we completely grasp the reality that we could lose them in an instant—with no warning and no opportunity to say good-bye. Although we all know this on some level, most of us seldom think about it. We're with our partner so much that it can be easy to slip into the habit of no longer seeing them as the lovable human being we once knew them to be.

One powerful way to maintain your appreciation for your partner is to intentionally focus on what life would be like if he or she weren't there. Take a moment to contemplate the loss you'd feel if your loved one were suddenly taken from you. Imagine getting the phone call and hearing the voice tell you that your partner has been in a serious accident and has just died. See this all as happening *right now.*

Now think back to any ways in which you've taken your partner for granted. This could be as simple as not noticing the everyday things they do for you or complaining or feeling disappointment about the way they do them. Then imagine how you would feel if he or she had really just died and how your life would unfold from this point forward. Make your mental images as realistic as possible, all the while feeling for the depth of your love for this incredible human being and all you've shared together.

This visualization quickly strips away the unimportant details of your relationship—the resentments, the expectations, and the other stuff that's accumulated between you—and leaves you with the essence of your connection. Through this practice, you will cultivate gratitude for your relationship and be less likely to waste the opportunities you have right now. This is especially true when you realize that this visualization will give you only a hint of what it would really be like to lose your loved one.

Knowing that visualization is a powerful practice for manifesting our desires, some people fear that imagining the worst will eventually bring it about. In this visualization, though, note that your focus is not on manifesting particular experiences or possessions. Your focus is on raising your awareness and appreciation of what you already have, so *appreciation* is what you will manifest.

> Jealousy
> is a negative way
> of looking at
> the possibility
> of losing someone.
> Appreciation
> is a positive way
> of looking at
> the very same thing.

Use this visualization to transform your experience of jealousy into one of gratitude. When you feel jealousy coming on, rather than feeding it with more jealousy-producing thoughts, focus on your visualization. Put your attention on your feelings of appreciation for having this human being in your life. Get in touch with how deeply you love this person and with how much this relationship deserves to be cherished.

Sharon and Daniel have been married for three years. Daniel's daughter, Emma, attends high school in a neighboring state. Daniel sees his daughter frequently, typically making the two-hundred-mile drive on Friday and returning late Saturday. At first Sharon was jealous about these trips. She intensified her feelings with thoughts like "He always puts Emma first. He only spends Saturdays with me if she has something else to do."

When Sharon decided that she wanted to let go of her jealousy over this issue, she made a promise to herself that every time these feelings started up, she would focus instead on all the things she loved about her husband. Because she knew she wouldn't be having children with Daniel, she also used this opportunity to appreciate his "daddy" side. She'd think about what a loving father he was and how happy he was when he spent time with his daughter. In addition, she would contemplate what her life would be like without Daniel in it.

Sharon finds this approach very effective. "I feel so much love for Daniel when he's visiting his daughter now. It's infinitely better than spending the time feeling neglected and upset!"

CHANNELING JEALOUSY
INTO DESIRE

We can also transform the energy of jealousy by using it to increase the passion and desire in our relationship. When we're faced with something we believe is threatening—like the thought that our partner will leave us for someone else—our body responds by flooding our bloodstream with adrenaline. The heightened state of alertness this hormone puts us into is similar to the state of sexual arousal. With practice, we can learn to reinterpret the rush of adrenaline that's generated by jealousy as *excitement* and have it be a reminder of the passion that's underneath.

Eric likes to use the idea that someone else finds his partner attractive to connect with his own attraction to her. "When a guy's paying attention to my girlfriend and I start to feel jealous," he says, "I take another look at her, like it's the first time, and try to see and feel what he's seeing and feeling."

If you get good at this, a little bit of jealousy might even become something you look forward to. "I like being reminded what an interesting and sexy woman she is," Eric says.

Juliana practices turning jealousy into desire when she's out with her boyfriend. "When I let myself experience the jealousy that comes up when he's talking to another girl, I can feel my desire for him too."

Bryan, a wedding photographer, has a similar perspective. "When someone has an interest in my lover, it makes me see him in a new way, and I want to step it up."

Lauri, the ballroom dancer, has found another way to channel jealousy into desire. "I realized the comparison game just wasn't one I could win. So instead of being threatened by other women's beauty, I decided to be inspired by it—to enjoy it myself. I would think, 'Wow. She's beautiful. No wonder my partner likes looking at her. I like looking at her too!'"

APPROACHING JEALOUSY
AS A HEALING OPPORTUNITY

In a truly connected relationship, jealousy provides an opportunity to participate in one of the most profound healing experiences possible.

Remember, jealous feelings are an automatic response to thoughts of comparison, inferiority, or inadequacy: "You think she's prettier than I am." "If I were enough for you, you wouldn't need to flirt with anyone else." Thoughts like these make us feel threatened, even when in our hearts we know we're not.

Any jealousy that arises in us is an indication that we are still holding onto insecurities and limiting beliefs about ourselves. Transforming those beliefs with the assistance of a loving, supportive partner is an especially intimate experience. *Situations that draw out our jealous feelings are exactly what we need to identify and release our limiting beliefs.*

Helping each other heal from *anything* rewards our relationship with gratitude and love.

Craig and Samantha know firsthand about the profound healing that comes through dissolving insecurity and jealousy in the safe space of a loving relationship. Craig is a natural flirt. For the first five years of their marriage, Samantha says, "I wasn't comfortable with that, but I knew it wouldn't be good for our relationship to try and change him."

Then the couple was introduced to the idea that Craig's naturally flirtatious behavior could offer Samantha an opportunity to heal her insecurities. Though apprehensive, she was willing to try it out.

"The next time it came up was at a friend's house," she says, "when Craig ran into a woman he knew from college. Soon they were talking about all their old friends, and the jealousy came on strong. I immediately started paying attention to what I was thinking."

Samantha identified several thoughts that were triggering her insecurity: "She's cuter than I am." "Did they have sex?" "Is she interested in him?"

Later, at home, she shared her thoughts with Craig.

"What we realized," he says, "was that Samantha still had doubts about the strength of our connection."

Craig responded to this discovery by putting into words exactly what he felt made their marriage so special.

"I reassured Samantha that she is beautiful, sexy, and very important to me. I told her that while I did have a sexual relationship with Claire and still find her attractive, I have no interest in gambling on another relationship when I have such an incredible one already."

The couple then created a replacement belief for Samantha to use whenever she found herself feeling insecure: "Craig loves this incredible relationship we have."

"This reminder really helps me let go of my jealousy when it comes up," Samantha says. "When I use it, I immediately feel close to Craig again."

PROCEED WITH LOVE

The ideas that follow are intended for couples who want to explore on a more intimate level and whose relationship is strong and flexible enough to support that. These couples have created a safe, loving, supportive space. They look for ways to expand to include anything that comes up and allow it to contribute positively to their relationship. They have experience with helping each other identify and transform limiting beliefs.

If you and your partner have issues around jealousy or sexuality, or if you're still struggling with memories of past abuse, you may not be ready for these types of explorations. It's also possible that they simply won't interest you or feel right for you.

If the two of you are ready to experiment, do so with an intention to feel connected at every moment and to fully accept and support one another in the process. Approach anything that comes up, like insecurity or jealousy, with compassion and a desire to heal the underlying causes. Appreciate each other for being willing to step out of your comfort zones to deepen your connection. Finally, *have fun!* Enjoy the feeling of being so intimate with someone you love.

CONNECT THROUGH
YOUR ATTRACTIONS

Many of us believe that it's disrespectful to noticeably find other people attractive when we're out on a date. Holding this belief, however, often has the unintentional effect of putting up invisible walls between you and your partner. When your significant other isn't "allowed" to notice other people, they might go underground, hoping their sideways glances won't be detected. Or they might force themselves to keep their gaze on you and anything else considered acceptable, while the resentment gradually builds.

"You mean I'm just supposed to *let* my wife look at other men?" you might ask at this point.

Given that she's likely to be looking anyway, you may even want to *invite* her to look. How could this possibly benefit you? For one thing, it will enable you to be far more comfortable in situations that used to leave you anxious and insecure, because you'll be having a shared experience rather than a separating one. For another, she's sure to love hanging out with you.

Consider John, who says, "With my previous girlfriend, anytime I noticed an attractive woman I was accused of leering and not respecting her. Then I met Nicole. She's not only okay with my attention occasionally being diverted by other women; she's even points them out to me!"

You might also discover that it's liberating for *you* when your partner feels free to be themselves.

"A lot of guys think they have to hide whenever they want to check out a cute girl," Nicole says. "If a guy acts awkward when he sees someone he's attracted to, I feel awkward too. But if he's relaxed being himself around me, I'm relaxed too."

The exploration that follows will likely bring up some uncomfortable feelings. *Uncovering and healing painful emotions, memories, and fears is an essential part of the process,* so it's vital that you have created a safe, supportive relationship space. In this loving environment, you will be able to openly share your thoughts and feelings and, together, find ways to transform your experience.

Before you begin this exploration, you might create an intention for it. Make staying connected, not the exploration itself, your priority.

The next time you and your partner are in a restaurant or at a party, choose a good vantage point to observe the people around you. One at a time, take turns being the watcher. If you're the watcher, let your gaze move around the room naturally and allow yourself to notice whoever catches your attention. (We said "notice," not "stare at.") Because of our conditioning, looking at someone other than your partner for even just a moment can be challenging. Remember that your partner is willingly supporting you in relaxing that conditioning.

> **What do we experience when we stop putting energy into worrying about our partner's attractions? Freedom.**

When your partner is the watcher, simply focus on their face and be receptive. As they observe people around the room, be aware of what you're thinking and feeling, especially any negative messages you might be giving yourself. You may need to actively keep your attention on thoughts like "It's amazing to be doing something like this together" and let go of ones like "I'm not as pretty as she is."

When someone catches your partner's eye, you'll know it. To some degree, you'll be able to *feel* what he or she is feeling. If you really absorb that feeling, you'll find yourself connecting with your partner on a very intimate level.

If jealousy comes up, approach it as a healing opportunity. Together, turn your attention to identifying and releasing the beliefs that are the source of the jealousy.

Don't be surprised if you find this exercise quite liberating and even sensual. By pushing the relationship envelope and exploring new dimensions together, you will be recharging (and possibly supercharging!) your sexual connection.

CONNECT THROUGH
YOUR PREVIOUS EXPERIENCES

Our past experiences, like our present attractions, have the potential to greatly contribute to our relationship. Many of us, though, are uncomfortable hearing about our partner's previous lovers and sexual encounters. We may be inclined to judge our romantic and sexual experiences against theirs or to compare ourselves to their past lovers. We may be concerned if our partner expresses appreciation or affection for a former lover. Many couples, usually through an unspoken agreement, simply avoid the topic altogether.

Some people, while intrigued by their partner's previous intimacies and the idea of sharing their own, have either been conditioned to stay clear of the subject or don't think their partner would be receptive. Other people would be comfortable relating their own stories, but would rather avoid the insecurities that would surface if they listen to their partner's.

Because many of us tend to experience jealousy in these situations, we're often advised to be cautious about which experiences we share and how much we reveal. We're warned not to say anything that could make our partner feel inadequate or insecure.

> In a fully intimate relationship, everything can be shared because everything is okay.

But if we set up our relationships so that we must censor ourselves and try to anticipate and avoid whatever might trigger our partner's jealousy, we may never know the profound intimacy that's at the heart of a truly connected relationship.

When we have the tools and the intentions in place to heal any uncomfortable feelings that surface, sharing our past romances and sexual encounters with our lover can be a path to deeper intimacy. Revealing aspects of ourselves that we normally keep hidden, and exploring them with the person we love, is true intimacy. A safe, loving space is also an ideal environment for investigating and beginning to heal painful memories or lingering wounds from sexual experiences that were embarrassing, diminishing, or traumatic. Through this process, you might also be inspired to investigate them further with the help of a coach or counselor.

If you and your partner decide to try sharing your memories and experiences, it will
be a very personal process. When you're the
storyteller, you might paint a scene for your
partner by describing the setting and how
you were feeling. When you're the listener,
you might just offer your partner your loving

presence, listening fully and letting go of any opinions, judgments,
or agenda. Or you might ask questions that encourage your partner to explore the memory more deeply. Whatever approaches the
two of you take, have an intention to stay completely connected.
If uncomfortable feelings are triggered, turning your attention to
exploring and healing them can be a truly loving experience.

As you connect through your intimate stories, your relationship
circle will expand to embrace your previous experiences. Instead of
feeling separate from each other's past, you will be drawing on those
pasts to contribute to your present—together.

*Knowing how to approach jealousy in ways that actually bring
you and your partner closer together can alleviate
one of the most challenging issues in many relationships.
By learning how to transform jealousy into appreciation
and desire, and how to use it as a healing opportunity,
one day you may even come to welcome this powerful emotion.*

10

Playing Leapfrog

*People relating on a soulmate level can help each other
release limiting beliefs, heal their past, and rise above their
perceived limitations. Just as players in the children's game
of leapfrog support one another in moving forward, you and
your partner can inspire each other to recognize and unlock
your potential in every area of your lives.*

In our ongoing pursuit to live a happy, fulfilling life, we are all evolving in many directions at once. We may be actively developing
ourselves in areas such as our career, our health, or our self-worth.
We might be improving our relationship to money, food, aging,
exercise, or sex. At any point in time, each of us will be more evolved
in some areas than in others.

In a soulmate relationship, partners are uniquely qualified to guide
and support each other in this natural process of self-development.
Better than anyone else, your partner can see your untapped potential.

They can "hold a positive belief about you," Michael Naumer liked to say, "until the evidence shows up." They can see opportunities for you to grow and expand. They can also detect where insecurity, doubt, or other fears may be holding you back. Your partner doesn't even need to be more evolved than you in a particular area in order to offer you invaluable support and guidance.

In a very real sense, *a soulmate is your custom-made personal coach, spiritual teacher, and cheerleader, aware of your potential, as well as your limitations, in every aspect of your life.* As your personal coach, they keep you on track with your desires and aspirations. As your spiritual teacher, they guide you in the direction of your very best self. As your cheerleader, they offer regular encouragement, motivation, and inspiration.

Leapfrog is the process through which soulmates assist one another in taking the next leap toward their full potential.

LEAPFROG:
RELATIONSHIP AT A HIGHER LEVEL

People in a soulmate relationship view themselves and their partners as continually evolving beings. They lovingly help each other in their pursuit to become the best possible version of themselves. When one of them is inspired to expand in a particular direction, the other offers his or her full assistance and encouragement.

Recent research into successful long-term relationships confirms that when two people support and affirm each other in becoming their ideal selves, their relationship thrives. In honor of the great

Renaissance artist, the term "Michelangelo effect" has been coined to describe this phenomenon. Like sculptors who chisel away stone to expose the art that is hidden inside, partners playing leapfrog sculpt and promote each other to bring out their very best qualities.

Soulmates can see their partner as already having made their next leap.

Audrey and Stefan, who met online several years ago, talk about supporting each other in becoming the people they dream of being.

"Stefan is an amazing human being, and I know I'm in his life to make sure he sees that," Audrey says. "It's inspiring to see the person you love blossom and know you've had a hand in that."

"When I see how much desire Audrey has for me to be my best," Stefan adds, "it makes me want to do the same for her."

People relating on a soulmate level recognize that everyone evolves at their own pace. They know that their partner's progress in any particular area may be gradual. (This is especially true if a core belief or deep-seated issue from the past is involved.) They understand that sometimes, after exploring a particular topic, they will have to let it go for a while. As hard as it can be to resist the urge to accelerate the pace, soulmates know how to intuitively sense for another opening to present itself, a time when their partner is again ready for their loving assistance.

Just as in the children's game, *the joy of playing leapfrog is in the process.* As Stefan says, "Every time we explore something together, even if we've talked about it before, it's an incredibly rewarding experience."

The upward spiral of leapfrog creates an extraordinary bond. When you've taken a leap with your partner's help and then view them from your new perspective, you will be seeing them through the eyes of gratitude and love. That will inspire you to help them make *their* next leap.

Soulmates have no timeline for their partner's evolution.

WHAT LEAPFROG IS NOT

To understand leapfrog, it's essential to recognize the distinction between assisting your partner with sculpting their *own* highest vision of themselves and imposing *your* vision on them. Leapfrog isn't about pushing your partner in a direction they're not interested in traveling. It's not about insisting that your partner be who you think they should be or do what you think they should do. Instead, it means offering your back as support for them to use in advancing along a path of their *own* choosing.

Many relationships break down when one partner continually tries to improve or fix what they perceive as the other's problems or shortcomings. In addition to a natural resistance to being told what to do or what's best for them, the person being "helped" rarely feels that their partner is really supporting who they are and where they'd like to go.

Months after they broke up, Lydia still focused on Bob's unwillingness to change as being the primary reason their relationship ended. She couldn't see how much her insistence that she knew what was best for him had contributed to the difficulties they had in getting along.

Bob says, "It always seemed like Lydia thought she was more enlightened, so I should listen to her. But I never felt she took the time to understand where *I* was coming from."

Acting as your partner's coach, and getting on your partner's case, are two entirely different things!

If you're not sure what your partner's highest vision of themselves is, *ask.* Explore their greatest dreams and aspirations with them, as well as how you might support him or her in those pursuits.

That said, *when two people are really tuned in to one another, they are often able to envision possibilities for their partner that their partner hasn't yet envisioned for themselves.* If you see potential in your partner that they don't, and you have a receptive, loving space in which to explore anything together, offer your vision as a possibility. If nothing tangible comes from it, at least you will have planted an idea that may take form in the future.

WHAT MAKES LEAPFROG POSSIBLE?

The previous chapters offer practical tools for creating a more enlightened relationship. These tools, plus a few additional ingredients—responsibility, trust, willingness, and transparency—will foster an environment that makes playing leapfrog possible.

Responsibility

In most conventional relationships, people haven't yet realized they are the source of their own unhappiness. Instead they point a finger outward, putting the blame on other people and the world for the "bad" things that happen to them. Because of this, any assistance their partner offers them won't address the real source of their suffering: how they are choosing to interpret whatever is occurring in their lives.

Though our partner may temporarily help lessen our experience of suffering, they can't heal its true cause. *Real change is an internal process.*

In a soulmate relationship, both people continually make an effort to take responsibility for their own experience. They do this by remembering that their *interpretation* of whatever is happening around them is what creates their *experience* of it. (This idea is explored in Chapter 1.) Because they don't accuse or look to their partner to "fix the problem" or make things right, their partner feels free to offer their full support and assistance.

> **When you take responsibility for your own experience, you're also able to take full advantage of your partner's assistance.**

Trust

Like responsibility, trust is essential for making leapfrog possible. The trust we're talking about, however, is not in the limiting sense of "I trust you to do this; I trust you not to do that." You might recall that this kind of trust, which originates in fear, is really just control in disguise (see Chapter 5).

The trust that is the basis for leapfrog is an *expansive* trust. First, you trust that your partner is doing the best they can. For example, if your partner has freely chosen and declared a context for your relationship (see Chapter 6), you trust they will do their best to tap into its wisdom and follow its guidance. Even if your partner only remembers to use their context on occasion, you understand that this is simply the best they can do right now.

Second, you trust yourself to use everything that shows up in your life and in your relationship as an opportunity to grow. This means that you not only don't resist difficult situations, but you do your best to welcome and get the most from them.

If your soulmate sees a positive quality in you, trust that it's there.

Willingness

The kind of profound healing that's possible in a soulmate relationship requires a willingness to be vulnerable and open. Avoiding these things with your soulmate can stem from a lack of self-acceptance, a fear of the unknown, or simple insecurity—*all of which your soulmate can assist you with, if you'll let them.*

Receptivity to your partner, and a willingness to be vulnerable, are the keys to getting the most out of leapfrog. *To make substantial leaps, you have to be willing to completely give yourself over to your partner and to the process.*

"Whenever I think I'm protecting myself by hiding or running away from something," Audrey says, "Stefan finds a way to gently pull me back. He gets me to see that I really can open up to whatever it is that I'm afraid of."

"I'm not going to let her run away," Stefan explains. "Because, deep down, the Audrey I know doesn't *want* to run away. She just needs a little help in facing her fears."

Transparency

Leapfrog is most effective when the players are as transparent as possible. This means they do their best to communicate their full truth: their thoughts, fears, feelings, and desires. When two people are this connected, keeping something hidden may not even be an option.

"I feel that Audrey is my own personal truth serum," Stefan says. "When I'm with her, I have no desire to hold anything back. I really appreciate who she is that brings that out in me."

Audrey says, "Our trust in one another is so strong that we know whatever the other is trying to show us will be valuable. So we listen, even when it's hard. I may not be able to hear it the first time, the third time, or even the tenth time he tells me, but I'll always do my best to hear it."

OFFER EACH OTHER
A HIGHER POSSIBILITY

This book is filled with ways to shift your perspective in any area where you are limiting your own potential. Every one of these tools has the power to transform your experience. If you've been using even a few of them, you have already discovered that it's possible to make tremendous progress on your own.

Sometimes, though, we forget to use these tools, or we struggle when we try to put them into practice. This is especially true when we're facing a challenging or fear-producing situation, dealing with a past trauma, or being overly hard on ourselves. At times like these, it's difficult to remember these tools are available, much less apply them.

That's where leapfrog comes in.

When you're having trouble finding an effective approach to a particular issue, your soulmate can be your guide. Obviously this doesn't mean trying to fix the problem for you or insisting that you follow a certain course of action. It means exploring together to find ways to view and approach the situation from a higher perspective.

Take Keith, an entrepreneur involved in an Internet startup. He and his two business partners are in the process of raising several million dollars by persuading potential investors that their idea is a promising one. There are times when the intensity of the high stakes gets to him.

"When I start to have doubts about the project, Katrina gets me back on track," Keith says. "First she reminds me that my nerves are normal and that no matter what happens, I'll learn a lot and apply that knowledge to my next project if this one doesn't work out. She helps me figure out

> Your partner can see possibilities for you when fear is preventing you from seeing them yourself.

what's causing my doubts—usually some kind of belief that I'm not capable of doing something so big. And she helps me remember all the reasons I really *am* capable, like the fact that I've managed large projects before and that I have an ability to see the big picture."

By offering you a higher possibility, such as inviting you to see yourself in another way, your soulmate can help you heal limiting or self-defeating beliefs. Because you have faith in your partner's ability to see aspects of yourself that you can't, you know there's value in whatever they have to say. You *want* to hear and try out their suggestions. When your soulmate invites you to see something about yourself that you haven't been seeing, didn't know was there, or forgot was there, you're open to their perspective.

Maya, a marketing manager in her fifties, sometimes gets down about the fact that she is aging. "Some days I look in the mirror and can't see anything but new wrinkles," she says.

Her partner, Anthony, helps Maya rise above the limited perspective of herself that she's caught up in at those times. "She has so much energy and enthusiasm, and she takes great care of herself," he says. "If I can help her to see what *I* see in her—a beautiful, ageless woman—she would radiate that all the time."

Anthony begins by getting Maya to recognize that these feelings arise when she focuses exclusively on how she looks. "I ask her how old she actually *feels,* and she says in her thirties or early forties."

"He's right," Maya says. "If I didn't know how old I was, I'd think I was a lot younger."

Anthony then helps Maya find ways to accept the person who's looking back at her in the mirror. "He gets me to see that I feel bad when I look at myself with the idea that I'm not as attractive as I used to be," Maya says. "He helps me find a more positive thought to focus on, like, 'My enthusiasm for life inspires others.'"

> When your partner is offering you a higher possibility, listen with the part of you that's most evolved.

Leapfrog is ideal for helping us free ourselves from unwanted habits or patterns. Johanna, for example, knew her abrupt way of saying things sometimes made other people feel small. She'd been trying to give up the habit for years. When she started dating Rafael, she told him about her desire to be more aware of her tone of voice. He came up with a simple, loving reminder to use when he heard her making comments that others might find harsh: He'd lean over and whisper "Ouch!" in her ear.

"It makes me smile, and then it's easy to shift my attitude," Johanna says.

Rafael's approach could also be used with someone who wants to break any unconscious habit, such as a tendency to complain or gossip.

In addition to helping us transform limiting beliefs, leapfrog can assist us in working with or even resolving lingering issues from the past. Your soulmate can help you find the higher possibilities in your experiences so that you can embrace your past and put all you've been through to its best possible use. In fact, you might find this process so empowering that you actually start to *search* for things in your past to explore together.

DESIGNING EXPERIENCES
TO HELP YOUR PARTNER LEAP

When you're encouraging your partner to take their next leap, often just talking about other possibilities with them will be all that's necessary. But words alone are not always enough. Sometimes our partner needs to actually *feel* themselves being the person we know they have the potential to be.

In this case, you might come up with exercises to help your partner dissolve the roadblocks they are putting in their own way. For example, if they are being limited by an anxiety or phobia, you could create experiences to help them explore

When you're offering
your partner
a higher possibility,
speak to their
most evolved self.

that fear. By approaching the issue from different angles, you can assist them to slowly free themselves from it.

When Keith and Katrina first met, Keith was extremely uncomfortable in social situations: "I was pretty much petrified by the thought of meeting new people."

Katrina could see, though, that her new love had the potential to be much more at ease with strangers. "He has a lot to offer, and I knew I could help him let go of whatever was holding him back." She'd seen him open up and be warm and authentic with people he'd known only a short while, once he'd gotten past the introductions. She knew that if she could help him over that barrier, the rest would be easy.

They began by identifying and addressing some of the beliefs that were underlying Keith's fear of social situations, like "I won't have anything to say" and "People will think I'm boring." They talked about how he felt when he contemplated going to a party, what he tended to do and think once he was there, and what it might look like for him to be relaxed in a group of people he didn't know. This helped give Keith a new image of who he could be.

Katrina then began to initiate conversations with strangers when they went out. "There was no expectation that I join in," Keith says, "but after a while, I started to relax. I didn't get nearly as nervous as I would have in the past."

They eventually transitioned into having Keith start up these conversations. "Knowing that Katrina was next to me," Keith says, "I could talk to strangers and be okay about feeling nervous. The more we practiced, the less I found myself wanting to avoid new situations. Now I actually *like* the challenge of starting a conversation with people I've just met. I still get nervous, but there's a feeling of excitement that goes along with that."

> Honor your partner
> by endeavoring
> to see in yourself
> everything he or she
> sees in you.

Audrey and Stefan also enjoy finding ways to help each other get over personal hurdles. "When he sees there's some way I'm holding myself back, he immediately goes after it!" Audrey laughs.

Although Audrey loves to dance when she's by herself, she'd never felt comfortable doing so in public. "I was self-conscious, always worried what the people around me would be thinking."

Even though Stefan isn't much of a dancer himself, he knew he could help. After a while, he was able to coax Audrey into dancing while he was in the room. "I suggested that if she'd focus on the music and the feeling of it in her body, she'd forget all about me being there."

"I practiced letting the music express itself through me while he was watching," Audrey explains, "without thinking about what I looked like."

"I realized that was key," Stefan adds. "How she feels, not how she looks."

Eventually Audrey felt ready to go out in public. "When a song I liked came on, we got up," Audrey says. "Stefan told me to hold his hands and look into his eyes. He said I didn't even have to move! But it didn't take long before I got into the music and let go of my fears about how I looked."

"Now she even sometimes *asks* me to watch her dance," Stefan reports. "It's so fun to see her really get into it!"

Leila and Brendon, who have been dating for a couple of years, also use leapfrog to assist each other. Brendon's favorite pastime is riding his motorcycles. He belongs to a club and participates in riding events a couple of times a month. Even though he's an experienced rider and Leila really wanted to join him on these adventures, she'd always been terrified of motorcycles.

"A lot of people think riding is just plain dangerous, and I understand that," she says. "But this is my boyfriend's passion, and I wanted to be able to share it with him."

Brendon knew that Leila would be safer if she were more

comfortable. "She'd grab me so tightly that *I'd* get nervous, and that's no way to ride," he says.

So they created their own "how to ride" course. Brendon began by acquainting Leila with the bike: its features, where to put her hands and feet, how to get on and off. They got her proper safety equipment, and she spent time becoming familiar with it. They talked about how to lean with him during turns. They also came up with signals: A tap on his left thigh meant slow down; a tap on his right meant she was feeling comfortable.

Sometimes it's your turn to expand; sometimes it's your partner's.

They began riding regularly on clear days, taking less-traveled back roads. "After just a short while," Brendon said, "I could sense even before she signaled that she was getting tense, and I'd slow down." He continued to modify his riding to match her comfort level, and Leila learned to relax and trust him. "In the process, I actually became a better rider myself," Brendon reports. "More in touch with my passenger. Which means it's safer for both of us."

PLAYING LEAPFROG
IN SUPPORT OF A SHARED CONTEXT

Whether they call it leapfrog or not, couples often use this same process to support shared relationship contexts (see Chapter 6).

Amy and Jeff have a shared context for raising their two daughters. "We want our children to be aware that we're not the only people on this planet," Amy says. "Our world is bigger than us, our neighborhood, or even what's important to us."

In the spirit of this context, the couple had a desire for their family to experience life in a foreign country. When they were offered an opportunity to live and work in Ghana for a year, Amy says, "We knew that the only way we could go on such an adventure was to really commit to being each other's support system. So we made an agreement to remind each other when things got difficult that this is a year for growth and we're here to take advantage of it. We don't want to waste that time suffering."

Jeff and Amy understood that suffering is what is produced when we resist what's happening in our lives. Reminding each other of this made it much easier for the couple to weather the social isolation, environmental issues, and unexpected job stress they encountered in Ghana.

"We'd actually say to each other, 'I understand that it's hard, and that you're in some kind of distress right now, but remember: You don't have to suffer.'"

Howard and Jenna each have a child from a previous marriage, and they also have one together. To make sure all three children feel they're an essential part of this blended family, the couple created this shared context: "Our family is loving and complete."

In support of this context, Jenna and Howard assist each other in building and maintaining positive relationships with their ex-spouses, as well as having loving relationships with each of their children. This includes being flexible and creative about holiday and vacation plans and fostering an environment that promotes connection with all of the important people in the children's lives.

"This communicates to our children that family is about people loving each other," Howard says. "Understanding this will help them establish strong, healthy relationships in the future, no matter what circumstances they find themselves in."

REMEMBER THAT LEAPFROG
IS ABOUT THE EXPERIENCE

When you're playing leapfrog, you might occasionally find your-self a little frustrated with your partner's progress. If so, don't be discouraged. Instead, look to see whether your *enthusiasm* for the higher possibility you're holding out has turned into an *expectation* that your partner make a certain amount of progress in a certain period of time.

If you see you do have some expectation or agenda about how fast, or even if, your partner progresses, remind yourself that, like everyone else, your partner is evolving at the pace that is perfect for him or her.

Your partner won't always want to play leapfrog when you want to—and that's okay! The key is to develop an awareness of when your partner *is* ready to play. You do this by letting go of any expectations and paying attention to your intuition.

> Watch children playing leapfrog and you'll see they're not trying to get anywhere.

213

When your partner is ready to play again, remember that, like the children's version of the game, there's nowhere in particular you have to get to. Leapfrog is all about the experience, not the result. You don't have to make a certain amount of progress for it to be rewarding. You're playing for the *fun* of it.

The loving, supportive environment of a soulmate relationship opens up new possibilities for relating on higher and higher levels. Acting as one another's personal coach, spiritual teacher, and cheerleader, you and your soulmate will be rewarded with the immense satisfaction that comes from witnessing each other evolve into your very best selves. The gratitude that arises through this process of leapfrog will certainly contribute to your ever-growing love and appreciation for each other.

11

Exploring the Edges

Every living thing on earth is continually changing.
Growth and change, in fact, are the essence of what it means to be
alive. So if you want a relationship that is fully alive, you have
to allow, and even encourage, growth and change—in yourself, in
your partner, and in your relationship. The trick is to continually
breathe new life into your relationship in ways that are both
fun and exciting as well as loving and connected.

After living together for three years, Katherine and Alex found themselves in the therapist's office. Katherine told the therapist that she often felt unheard and underappreciated. Alex said that Katherine frequently came across as cold and dismissive. They were both concerned that the passion between them was fading away, and they were growing weary of the constant effort of trying to make their relationship work. Katherine was even thinking of calling off their engagement.

The therapist suggested that the couple begin to address their feelings of disconnection by adding a simple routine to their lives. Every night before going to bed, they would each make a list of what they had appreciated about the other that day. Focusing on their appreciation for one another would only take a few minutes, she said, and would help keep their romance alive.

That evening, Katherine was eager to share her list with Alex. She excitedly read him ten ways she had felt appreciation for him that day.

Then she looked up. "So what's on *your* list?"

"Nothing," Alex mumbled. "I didn't make a list."

Alex found he simply couldn't express his gratitude on command. "I love Katherine, and there's *lots* I appreciate about her. But being told I have to put that into words *right now* just paralyzed me."

Feeling and expressing gratitude is one of the most powerful ways to enhance your relationship experience. If both partners enjoy setting aside time to share their appreciation for each other, it's a ritual that will certainly strengthen their connection. However, in Alex and Katherine's case, the suggestion inadvertently added another layer of expectation onto an already strained relationship. Along with that expectation, of course, came the usual frustration, guilt, and resentment.

True appreciation won't arise out of expectation. If you hold an expectation that someone should appreciate you, that "expectation energy" actually has the potential to shut down the free flow of appreciation.

If scheduling time to share his appreciation for his fiancée won't work, how might Alex learn to show his gratitude more often? He could start by paying attention to when he is naturally feeling appreciation for Katherine and get in the habit of expressing it right then.

Another common piece of advice for keeping a relationship vibrant is to establish a weekly date night. Couples devote one night a week to being together so they can concentrate on and enjoy their relationship. This is considered especially helpful for partners who feel their relationship is taking a backseat to their day-to-day responsibilities.

Spending quality time together can certainly help a relationship thrive, and many couples have found that establishing a date night helps ensure they get that time together. For others, though, date night creates a feeling of obligation and can become a potential source of resentment and guilt. Some couples actually feel the pressure between them increase. They know they're supposed to be looking forward to the evening, whether they're feeling up to it or not. If they try to get out of the date, they're likely to face their partner's disappointment: "I thought we made an agreement about this. We can't cancel every time one of us is tired."

> Romance is rarely rekindled through obligation or expectation.

As Tom, who is in couples' counseling with his wife, expressed it, "It sounded like a great idea at first. But there's a big difference between *wanting* to have a date night and *having* to have a date night."

SO WHAT *WILL* KEEP
A RELATIONSHIP ALIVE?

You probably know couples in long-lasting relationships who are genuinely content with and appreciative of the life they have together. But after being together a while—especially with the added challenges of financial issues or raising a family—many couples feel their relationship becoming boring or even lifeless.

Michael Naumer often observed that relationships typically "begin as an expansion and then start to contract." When we base our relationships on the conventional model and attempt to protect and preserve them to keep them from changing, contraction is the inevitable result. When we base our relationships on the soulmate model, with freedom as a guiding principle,

> A relationship
> that continually expands
> is alive.

we encourage that process of expansion to continue. *Allowing ourselves and our relationships to continually expand, even in small ways, will help keep our connection energized.*

If you practice yoga, you may have heard your teacher talk about "finding your edge." In the physical sense, your edge is the place where you're getting a really good stretch but not so much that you're overstretching and pushing into pain. You always have an edge, even if you've been practicing for thirty years. Your edge in this moment isn't the same as it was yesterday, and it won't be the same tomorrow. It's certainly not the same as that of the person next to you.

Once you've found your edge, you breathe into it, using your breath to expand those muscles just a little bit more. As you continue to breathe into that area, you feel your body opening up from the inside. This practice of tuning into your body and becoming aware of the places where you are able to expand is called "playing at your edge."

To expand in your relationship, as in yoga, learn to play at your edge.

Which brings us back to date night. The time we spend together tends to lose its luster when we go on autopilot and let our daily routine become our whole life. By engaging in new experiences and expanding in new ways—*by playing at the edges*—our relationship will continue to grow and change. In other words, our relationship is alive.

IT'S NOT A DATE
—IT'S AN EXPERIENCE

Recent research into long-term relationships confirms that *novelty* is essential for sustaining romance. Exciting new experiences cause the body to produce the same hormones that are activated when we fall in love. When we encounter the unknown, we enter a state of heightened awareness. We feel *alive*. And when we do this together, we feel connected through that sense of vitality.

By intentionally looking for ways to play at the edges, you'll inject some of these hormones into date night—breathing life into both your dates *and* your relationship. You'll find that fifteen minutes of playing at your edges can be far more stimulating than a typical four-hour "dinner and a movie."

Exploring the edges will look different for every couple. Just as each individual grows and evolves in his or her own way, so does every relationship. Some of the suggestions here will entice you, while others may seem silly or even scary. What you're looking for are activities that have the potential to increase the intimacy and connectedness between you and your partner.

One way to inject novelty into your relationship—and make date night compelling as well as fun—is to experiment with activities that are entirely new to you both. The range of experiences available today is virtually unlimited. With ten minutes of research online (try searching "exciting date ideas" or listings of local events), you'll find plenty of ideas for things that will make you both a little nervous or apprehensive—which is exactly what you're looking for.

One secret to keeping your relationship exciting is to stretch your comfort zones.

You might take a class together, like contra dancing, painting, singing, partner yoga, or couples massage. Join a drum circle, go out for an evening of karaoke, volunteer at a hospital or homeless shelter, or shoot a game at the local pool hall. Attend an experimental music concert, a performance art show, or a lecture on a topic you know nothing about. Be spontaneous: Climb a tree, do a cartwheel, walk in the rain, make out in the moonlight. Read poetry to each other, go bowling, join a book group, or take a photography walk. Challenge your inner skeptic by visiting a palm reader, having your aura photographed, or getting a tarot reading. Camp out instead of reserving a room—especially if you've ever insisted, "I don't camp!" Remember, *the point is to go beyond your comfort zones.*

Physical activities, particularly unfamiliar ones, are especially bonding, as they will call on you to support and rely on one another. Take a hip-hop or tai chi class. Try hula hooping, skinny dipping, line dancing, or indoor skydiving. Take lessons at a rock-climbing gym, join a boot-camp workout group, or train for a triathlon. Or get a little more intimate by seeking out a Japanese spa, a mud bath, or even a pole-dancing class. If these suggestions are too mundane for you, how about stripping down for a naked yoga class?

Try designing some date experiences around the senses. If you're lucky enough to live near a city with a restaurant that serves meals in the dark, reserve a table. Find some live music—and listen with your eyes closed. Rent a couple of sensory-deprivation tanks for an hour. Go on a speech fast for an evening, which will inspire you to communicate in other ways. (Yes, it is possible to order dinner without talking!) Or take an excursion where each of you walks sightless for a while. If you're the one being led, put your trust in your partner and your full attention on your senses. Describe the sounds, smells,

When you try new experiences together, you can't help but have a new experience of each other.

and sensations you're noticing. If you're leading, you might guide your partner deeper into the experience by asking, "What are you feeling? What do you hear? How does the air feel on your skin?"

Or arrange a "first date" by taking on the roles of two single, independent people. If you do this successfully, you'll experience some of the allure and mystery of a new encounter. Set the stage by traveling separately to a place neither of you has ever been; an unfamiliar location will help create that "first date" feeling. Rather than waiting for your partner to show up, go in and find a seat. When you do meet, look at your date through the eyes of someone who doesn't already know them. If you become aware that you're making any assumptions or judgments, let them go and concentrate instead on what you find intriguing or attractive about this person. Make eye contact. Flirt with them. *Be seductive.* If you can stay in your roles throughout dinner and all the way home, there's a good chance you'll be making love to someone new tonight.

Another out-of-the-ordinary date experience involves each of you taking on a new identity and showing up in character, right down to your names. You might choose a career you've always had a secret longing for: This is your chance to be that famous novelist, celebrity, or renowned winemaker. Or pick something totally out of character, like a UFO researcher, an international spy, or even a hired escort!

Emily and Adam, who have been married for several years, love getting creative with their dates. One of them will arrange something unique—an evening of stargazing, a swim in a nearby lake, a romantic stroll at sunset, or Thai massages for two—and tell the other only what's necessary.

Adam tells the story of a birthday experience he planned for Emily. Before they pulled out of the driveway, he tied a silk blindfold over her eyes. "After a few minutes in the car, I lost all sense of direction," Emily recalls. "As Adam led me to the restaurant, I heard a little girl playing, and we stopped to talk to her. She was so animated and happy—it was an incredible experience to try to picture her just from the sound of her voice. I almost couldn't resist the urge to take off my blindfold! And I can't tell you how delicious the food tasted that night."

Observers are much more likely to be intrigued than judgmental when they see how much fun you're having!

Emily and Adam relate another experience that is more personal. Both of them had always been uncomfortable being undressed around other people. When Emily jokingly suggested they go to a clothing-optional spa, Adam initially cringed. But he quickly recognized it as a good idea. Because they had both avoided nudity in the past, Adam realized this was the perfect opportunity to support each other by facing their fears together.

"We were so nervous we almost turned around on the way in," Emily says. "Although the first few minutes of walking around naked in front of other people had us both sweating like crazy, the whole adventure turned out to be way more fun than scary. We've even been back several times since."

Emily and Adam say these kinds of experiences keep their relationship exciting.

"In my previous marriage," Adam says, "we never explored the edges; the relationship was dull and dying. Now I understand that the edges are where the life is."

USE INTENTION
TO GUIDE YOUR EXPERIENCES

Whenever you're exploring the edges together, it can be beneficial to first take a few minutes to tune into each other and create an intention for the experience. For example, if you're trying something new, like a contact yoga class, or going to a party where one or both of you might feel a little nervous or jealous, you might explicitly make an intention to stay connected throughout the experience.

When Emily and Adam spent that first weekend at a clothing-optional spa, they each set their own intention for the experience. Emily's was to feel her body as a whole instead of dwelling on any specific part. Adam's was to practice relaxing while he was interacting with people who weren't wearing clothes.

On another occasion, when they attended a free-form dance, Adam went in with the intention of simply allowing himself to move to the music without worrying that he might look awkward. Emily's intention was to not compare herself to other women and to remind herself as often as necessary that she was just fine the way she was.

> An intention
> is an energetic
> game plan
> that helps to
> shape and guide
> your experiences.

In addition to regularly creating intentions, both shared and individual ones, Emily and Adam sometimes use a simple visualization to enhance their connection. "When we went to the free-form dance, where everyone dances with everyone else, we imagined a gold cord connecting the two of us the whole time," Emily explains. "It really helped me feel like we were together, especially when Adam was on the other side of the dance floor."

CONNECT THROUGH YOUR EXPERIENCES

Keeping your relationship vibrant by exploring the edges is about more than merely having a good time together. It's about using everything you experience to connect on deeper, more meaningful levels.

Commit to getting all you can from each new experience. Take a moment beforehand to share your fears or concerns as well as any feelings of anticipation or excitement.

During the exploration, do your best to open up to each other. The more you and your partner are in touch with what both of you are feeling, the more of a shared adventure it becomes. Allow yourself to fully experience any excitement, fear, or nervousness you feel, and find ways to communicate those feelings. Also be receptive to everything that is coming up for your partner. Really *be there* with them.

Claudia, a college professor, attended a tantra workshop with her girlfriend. At some point during one of the exercises, a feeling of panic swept over her.

"I wasn't sure what to do," Claudia recalls. "For a few moments I tried to cover it up, but it was overwhelming. When I confessed to Kaye that I was feeling really scared, she put her arms around me and held me. At that moment I felt closer to her than I ever had before."

SUPERCHARGE YOUR DATES
WITH LEAPFROG

Leapfrog takes dating to a whole new level. Keep your eyes open for a limitation your partner is ready to break through, a talent they're ready to own, or a fear they're ready to overcome. Use your imagination—and your love for them—to create experiences that will encourage them to grow in that area.

Josh had been raised by a father who had a habit of making derogatory comments about gay men. Intellectually, Josh had no issues with homosexuality, but he still found himself uncomfortable around gays. His girlfriend, Hilary, sensed that his uneasiness was something he was ready to be free of. So one day, on her suggestion, they headed for the gay neighborhood in a nearby city.

Josh admits to some nervousness when Hilary led him into a hip men's clothing store. But before he knew it, they were both laughing at the salesman's lighthearted teasing and everyone in the store was offering fashion suggestions.

"Looking back on it, being the center of attention in a gay clothing store was a pretty fun experience," Josh says. "From that point on, my awkwardness around gay men just evaporated."

Designing a date around leapfrog can result in an incredibly connected adventure—and a very grateful partner!

"And he dresses with a lot more style these days," Hilary says with a smile.

PLAYING LEAPFROG
IN THE BEDROOM

When two people have a close, intimate physical connection and complete trust in one another, they can use leapfrog to help each other break through negative beliefs about their bodies and their sexuality, even if those beliefs are long-standing. This emotional healing process is deeply personal and profoundly freeing. It opens the couple up to experiencing even more love in their relationship, both through the healing experience itself and through the freedom it offers them to explore and enjoy their physical connection on an even deeper level.

Hilary and Josh were willing to share one such intimate healing experience in the hope that other couples might find it inspirational. Josh designed this experience to help Hilary finally release a belief she'd been holding: that her breasts were too small.

"Intellectually, Hilary knew it was a waste to spend any more time thinking that way," Josh says. "But she just couldn't let go of the idea that she was insufficient in the breast department."

Because the four ingredients that make leapfrog possible—responsibility, trust, willingness, and transparency—were all present, the environment was perfect for Josh to assist Hilary in making this leap. So one Saturday, Josh told Hilary they were going to devote the day to her breasts.

"She resisted at first," he says. "But she knew this would be a positive, loving experience, and she eventually trusted herself to me."

227

Josh began the morning by leading Hilary into the bathroom, where he turned on the shower. He asked her to step into it and focus on enjoying the feeling of the warm water on her skin. After a few minutes, he began to talk to her.

"I reminded her that she was beautiful to me exactly as she was. Then I had her close her eyes and put her hands on her breasts while the water ran over her. I asked her to imagine that she'd never felt her breasts before, and to notice how soft and sensuous they were."

"The weird thing was," Hilary recalls, "my breasts actually *felt* different, and even a little larger than I'd been imagining them."

After this, Josh says, "I asked her to move her hands from her waist up and over her breasts and to notice how perfectly they complemented her body."

Later, Josh talked with Hilary about the idea that when she compared her breasts with society's ideal size, she would always feel inadequate. "I reminded her that while it's true that millions of people are drawn to larger breasts, it's just as true that millions find small breasts sexy and attractive. So if she was going to be concerned about what other people thought, she might as well focus on those who *are* attracted to smaller breasts."

Once Hilary could begin to recognize that her breasts were beautiful in their own way, Josh had her pick out a variety of outfits, from casual to dressy, and model them. In each one, he asked her to look at herself in the mirror and find something attractive about her breasts. He also pointed out what his attention was drawn to, like the sexy curves that disappeared into the fabric.

"He was so lovingly insistent," Hilary says. "At some point, I realized that my breasts really are, well, sweet."

Josh took photographs of her in each outfit. "After that, of course, he had me pose naked!" Hilary laughs.

Being naked was more challenging for Hilary than wearing clothes. "But when I found myself judging the size of my breasts again, I'd hold them and close my eyes, and reconnect with that feeling of them being sweet. Once I did that, I was able to really be myself in front of the camera."

Later, while Hilary relaxed in the bath, Josh created a slide show of the photographs they'd taken. When they watched it together, he had her imagine that she was seeing someone she didn't know.

"It was amazing," Hilary says. "When I looked at the pictures as though it was some other woman, I liked them so much more! I realized that my self-rejection was getting in the way of seeing how I actually look."

That evening, Josh asked Hilary to dress in something that she felt made her breasts look particularly attractive. When they went out, he had her focus on staying in touch with her appreciation for her breasts and on enjoying how truly beautiful they were.

"When Josh made love to me that night," Hilary says, "it was as though he was touching my breasts for the first time. Not only could I really enjoy them now, but I could let Josh enjoy them too."

Josh adds, "There's been a huge benefit for me too. When we're making love and I touch her breasts, her whole body responds. She *wants* me to touch her. I can't tell you the pleasure that brings me."

THE DAMAGE OF THE
DEFAULT NO

Most people, if asked, will say they're open-minded and receptive to trying new things. The truth is, however, many of us are carrying around an extensive collection of fixed beliefs about what we like and dislike and about how things should be. Michael Naumer used to put it this way: "People's default position for participation is generally no."

Kara, a real estate broker in her forties, considers herself to be a "yes, let's go for it!" kind of person. But in her most recent relationship, which lasted just four weeks, "no" quickly got in the way.

Kara says that the day she and Paul met, they connected on so many levels that she hoped it might be the start of something long-lasting. Then Paul asked her to a salsa dance, something he'd been enjoying weekly for more than a year. Kara found herself frustrated once the dancing began.

"We were supposed to rotate partners for every new dance," she says. "But I couldn't see spending every Friday night there and getting to be with Paul only two or three times. It was a definite deal-breaker. Too bad, because there aren't that many guys out there who interest me."

Kara, like many of us, is not nearly as open-minded as she imagines herself to be. She essentially issued a "default no" to Paul's passion for dancing. She rejected it without really investigating whether there was an approach to the situation that could enhance, rather than end, their relationship.

Kara and Paul might have chosen to do their own things most Friday nights, which would make their Saturdays that much more special. But Kara dismissed this idea because she felt it was important for a couple to spend most of their weekend evenings together. If she had considered that this belief is simply one of many possible ways to approach a relationship, she might have seen that it wasn't serving her particularly well.

Another approach Kara could have tried was to find a way to get something out of the Friday night dance. Dancing is good exercise, and as she improved, she'd no doubt enjoy it more. When she was there only to be with Paul, it wasn't very satisfying. But if she went to create an *experience* with Paul—like connecting with each person they danced with and sharing the highlights of their interactions later— she might even start to look forward to it.

Relationships with soulmate potential come around a lot more frequently than we might imagine. But we're often unable to recognize them because we have so many inflexible ideas about how they're supposed to look.

> The "default no" can severely limit a relationship's potential.

Monica, a hair stylist, describes her relationship with her last boyfriend, whom she lived with for two years: "Joel was wonderful in so many ways. But he snored all night long, and I happen to be a very light sleeper. The doctor said nothing could be done in Joel's case. It just wasn't going to work for me. I need to be able to sleep with my boyfriend *and* get the rest I need. So I finally had to move out. It was too bad, because we were compatible in every other way."

A few weeks after she ended the relationship, Monica met Alicia. Alicia was also a very light sleeper and, Monica learned, was living with a man who snored nightly. Monica was eager to hear how she handled the situation.

Alicia explained that she believed she could train herself to ignore her boyfriend's snoring. Each time it woke her, she reminded herself that it was just her lover sleeping next to her. After a couple of weeks, Alicia said, she was sleeping through the night. She'd still wake up when her daughter moved in the room down the hall, but her boyfriend's snoring rarely disturbed her.

After hearing Alicia's story, Monica says, "I sure wish I'd thought about this possibility at the time . . ."

Even if Alicia's idea hadn't worked for Monica, if she'd been more willing and receptive to finding an approach that did, she very well might have discovered one. She could have experimented with earplugs or a white noise machine. She might have helped Joel find another doctor to get a second opinion. Or she could have expanded her concept of an intimate relationship to include the idea that sleeping together all night is not a critical component of being together. *There are always other possibilities, when we're open to seeing them.*

RELATIONSHIP AS A CONSTANT YES

We're all passionate about something. Some of us are at our happiest laughing with friends, cooking a meal, or being in nature. Some of us feel most alive when we're doing something physical, like swimming, running, dancing, or rock climbing. We might have a passion for gardening, photography, classic movies, sailing, or poetry. Or we might find our greatest joy in simple rituals, like meditating, taking our dog for a walk, or sitting quietly with a cup of tea.

One of the most rewarding aspects of relationships is the ongoing opportunity to tap into and explore each other's passions. Though some people approach their partner's interests with an attitude of getting the most from them, others shrug them off with disinterest: "Yeah, he's really into his backpacking trips, but they just don't excite me." If you've never taken the time to really experience and appreciate something your partner is passionate about, you have a tremendous opportunity to enrich your relationship. That's because one of the easiest and most

Though someone else's interests may not seem exciting to you, the passion they experience through them is real.

rewarding ways to connect with someone is through what inspires them—especially when you ask them to act as your guide into that experience.

This doesn't mean you have to give up every weekend to wander around antique shops or play golf. It certainly doesn't mean crossing your own boundaries about what is healthy or harmful for you. It *does* mean being willing to take on your partner's interests from time to time by letting go of your resistance and preconceptions. It means exploring with an open mind. It means knowing that *if your partner experiences passion in this activity, the passion is there for you to experience, too.*

Adam grew up watching football, first with his dad and later with his college buddies. When he met Emily, she knew nothing about the sport and had never even seen a game.

"I do like sports," she says. "But being a spectator never interested me. It just seemed so pointless."

When Emily asked Adam to help her appreciate what he got out of watching a game, he was very enthusiastic: "None of my previous girlfriends had ever been interested!" So one Sunday they made a date to watch a game together. Adam focused on sharing with Emily everything he found intriguing about the sport. Emily did her best to tap into Adam's excitement and to let go of any negative thoughts that drifted into her head about the game.

"He told me about the sense of anticipation that comes on before a big game," Emily says, "and described how he follows the action without thinking about it much, just feeling the agility and power of these incredibly fit athletes. After a while, I could feel that too. I could really appreciate how watching a game is an escape for him after being 'on' all week at work."

Once you choose to experience your partner's passion, make a commitment to yourself to get all you can out of it. Do your best to let go of your expectations about how it will be. Remember, the beliefs you hold will strongly influence your experience. So be on alert for any thoughts that what you're doing is silly, boring, or a waste of time: "I don't see how I'm going to get very excited about this art show." "I've tried this before. I didn't like it then; why would I like it now?" If you go into an experience with ideas like these, your mind will find evidence to support them, and *you'll produce exactly the experience you expect.*

When you're sharing your passion, be your partner's personal guide into the experience. Let go of any thoughts of the "she's not really interested in this" variety. Put your focus on finding ways to express what you're feeling, what you appreciate, and what intrigues you. Be grateful for your partner's willingness to experience this activity or interest with you—whether they ever choose to do so again or not.

One of Emily's favorite pursuits is trying new cuisines. "When Adam and I first met, though, he much preferred burgers and pizza," she says. To encourage him to expand his palate, they played a game where they would taste foods at the same time.

No matter what your partner's passion is, there's something to discover in the passion *itself.*

Emily would do her best to put into words exactly what she enjoyed about each one—the texture, a certain flavor, or a feeling the food conjured up—and Adam would search for what she was describing.

"I've realized that her experience of any particular food is as real as mine," Adam says, "so I've learned to let go of my automatic 'I don't like it' reaction. Now I like pretty much everything she likes."

As you practice watching for your "default no" and transforming it into a "constant yes," you might be surprised to discover that you really are able to enjoy things you previously thought you couldn't. Soon you might even find yourself asking, "What great things am I going to get from saying yes this time?"

EXPLORING THE EDGES
IN EVERYDAY LIFE

Exploring the edges is about more than bringing an adventurous spirit to date night. It's also about all those times in between date nights, when you're just living life: taking care of the kids, paying the bills, or making dinner. It's about inviting that connected, loving energy into every facet of your life together and allowing *all* your experiences, from the routine to the challenging, to contribute something positive to your relationship.

> A soulmate relationship isn't so much about *what you do* as it is about the *spirit* in which you do it.

This idea, in fact, is the single greatest secret to keeping your soulmate experience alive—a secret that can be summed up in one sentence:

Your relationship will *be* fully alive when you continually explore what makes it *feel* fully alive.

Exploring the edges is about approaching everything—even those things you encounter every day—as an opportunity for intimacy and growth. It's about being receptive to and even seeking out new ways to connect as you expand yourself and your relationship. At its heart, exploring the edges is about cultivating a love for life.

12

Connecting on a Soul Level

How you choose to relate to and interact with the people and situations you encounter every day profoundly influences the experiences you will have. Each of the five practices presented in this chapter is a fundamental choice you can make about how to approach your life. These five choices—which are the foundation for every idea in this book—are at the very heart of connecting on a deeply intimate level with another human being. The more you incorporate these practices into your life, the more harmonious and fulfilling your relationships will become.

By now you may have realized that every idea in this book is based on the simple truth that *who we are in our relationships is our choice.* Whether it's the way we approach expectation, resentment, or jealousy, or how we treat our partner or ourselves, our relationship experiences are largely shaped by the moment-to-moment choices we make.

The practices that follow are five simple ways you can respond to anything that comes up in your life and in your relationships. These basic choices have the power to transform every facet of your life. As you apply these practices more often, you will discover that there are opportunities all around you to connect with others on a profoundly intimate, soul-to-soul level.

The description of each practice includes suggestions for how to use it with another person. This might be your partner, a close friend, or even a stranger who's willing to take a risk and explore with you.

PRACTICE 1:
ACCEPT "WHAT IS"

Wherever you are, whatever you're doing, you have the choice to accept "what is" or to resist it.

Accepting "what is" right now doesn't mean you necessarily agree with or condone a particular situation or give up your ability to improve it. In fact, when you aren't stuck in resistance, you'll be in a much better place to assess and understand the situation and decide if and how to respond to it. Any action you *do* decide to take will be guided by wisdom instead of being driven by emotions like irritation, frustration, or anger.

In the same way, being receptive, non-judgmental, and open-minded toward others doesn't mean you necessarily agree with their opinions or approve of their actions. *Accepting another person simply means you recognize and acknowledge that this is who they're being at this moment.*

Actions and decisions made from a place of acceptance will be wiser than those made from a place of resistance.

238

Why is cultivating an attitude of acceptance so valuable in a relationship? Because *acceptance is what makes true intimacy possible.* When you aren't spending your limited time and energy in resistance, you will be more available for authentic, heart-to-heart connection.

Bring Your Awareness to Your Resistance

Although it's not always easy to do, you can learn to recognize when you're going into resistance, whether it's resistance to ideas, situations, events, or people.

Any time you hear yourself complaining, you can be sure you're resisting someone or something, whether it's your in-laws, your neighbors, or your job. The same is true whenever you're expressing some kind of judgment, criticism, or blame, either out loud or in your head. When you're in resistance to *yourself*, that persistent voice of your inner critic will bring on feelings of insecurity or doubt.

Even mild feelings of anxiety, irritation, boredom, and impatience are usually a sign that you're not accepting what is. In addition, any resentment you're holding onto is just your continued resistance to something that happened in the past.

> When you approach life from a place of acceptance, you naturally treat yourself and others with more love, compassion, and appreciation.

Simply noticing that you're in resistance will interrupt the thoughts that are the origin of your feelings. This gives you a little distance from the situation, allowing you to step back and take a look at what you're doing. You may then have enough awareness to ask yourself, *What are the possible benefits of accepting what I'm currently resisting?* This transformational question will help you move beyond a limited perspective. As your resistance starts to fall away, your perspective will expand and you will see possibilities for interpreting and responding to the situation that you couldn't see before.

Acceptance: The Direct Path to True Intimacy

Consciously practicing acceptance with another person can be a powerful, heart-opening experience. This practice is invaluable for going into a situation that is likely to trigger resistance in one or both of you, such as visiting a crowded tourist site, driving in heavy traffic, or doing chores.

For example, if you're at a party or other social event with a friend, you could both decide to watch for any reactions you have to the people you meet. Observe whether any opinions or negative judgments come up for you, and share with each other whatever you're getting out of the experience.

If you're in a relationship, you might try using this approach if one or both of you tend to get annoyed or exasperated when you visit family. On your next visit, arrive with an intention to practice accepting everyone exactly as they are: what they say, what they do, and how they do it. This means being totally okay with Uncle Jack retelling the same stories you've heard for years and Aunt Kate continually asking if you want more dessert.

Bringing your shared awareness to the situation will reward you with a significantly more enjoyable and meaningful experience with your relatives. You'll not only feel closer to them; you and your partner will feel closer to each other, as you'll be connecting through your mutual appreciation for having these people in your lives. You might even share a smile when Aunt Kate asks once again if you'd like another slice of pie.

PRACTICE 2:
BE RIGHT HERE, RIGHT NOW

In every moment, you have the choice to be right here, right now, or to be in the past or the future. When you spend time feeling guilty or resentful about things that happened in the past, or imagining or worrying about what might happen in the future, you simply can't fully experience what's happening right now.

Notice When You're Not in the Present

What does being present or in the moment really mean? It means having your attention on what you're experiencing *right now*, rather than allowing your mind to be overrun by thoughts about what happened yesterday or what might happen tomorrow. Being present means really tasting the food you're eating, really listening to the music you're hearing, and really experiencing the person you're with. It means being fully engaged in whatever you're doing.

By being observant of your emotional state, you can detect when you're not in the present. One sign that you're dwelling in the past is feelings of guilt, regret, shame, or resentment. Worry is an indicator that you're hanging out in the imaginary future. When unproductive or anxiety-producing thoughts about the past or the future come up, gently set them aside and refocus your attention on what's happening right now. For most of us, this is a lifelong practice, something we will get better at over time.

Another indication that you're not in the present is when your relationship begins to feel dull and lifeless. This may be a sign that you are relating to your partner through your *ideas* about them rather than seeing them as they really *are* in this moment. To keep your relationship feeling alive, stay open to who your partner is right now.

> The most valuable gift you can give is your presence.

Be Here Right Now—Together

Practicing being in the present with a friend or significant other will instantly make your time together more meaningful and authentic. You might go out to dinner with an intention to stay in the present as much as possible for that hour or two. Rather than thinking or talking about the past or the future, just be with each other. Absorb the atmosphere and your surroundings. Really see each other when you look, hear each other when you speak, and feel each other when you touch. Fully taste the food you're eating. If you notice that you're drifting into thoughts of resentment or worry, let them go and return your attention to the present.

If one of you slips into talking about the past or future, the other can gently move the conversation back into the present. You might even want to arrange in advance a simple signal to use as a gentle reminder for each other, like a squeeze of the hand.

When you're making love, helping each other to stay in the present will intensify your experience. If you find yourself distracted by thoughts about what you're going to do tomorrow, your partner might say to you, "Put your attention on the sensation of my hands on your skin, and let your thoughts fade into the background."

PRACTICE 3:
COME FROM A PLACE OF LOVE

We can classify nearly the entire range of human emotions into two categories: those that are generated when we're in a state of fear and those that are generated when we're in a state of love. In every moment, we have the choice to come from one or the other of these two states.

Doubt, anxiety, guilt, complaint, blame, and anger are all forms of fear, as are thoughts of comparison, inadequacy, and inferiority. Fear manifests as expectation, resentment, and jealousy. It is fear that compels us to be deceptive, controlling, critical, judgmental, manipulative, threatening, or possessive. We feel most disconnected from other people when we're coming from fear.

> Fear is
> the only thing
> that ever prevents
> two people from
> connecting.

Love, on the other hand, manifests as understanding, compassion, integrity, and honesty. It is love that compels us to be genuine, giving, encouraging, receptive, gentle, and accepting. We feel most connected to other people when we're coming from love.

You might recall that the conventional model for relationship is based to a great extent on fear. Afraid of losing what we have, we view certain people and situations as potential threats as we try to secure and protect our relationship to keep it from changing. As a result, our relationship will feel more and more closed down, or contracted, over time.

The soulmate model for relationship, in contrast, is based on freedom, which is one of the many manifestations of love. When we approach our relationships from a place of love, we welcome changes and challenges as they come. We look for ways to allow everything that happens to contribute to our experience. Consequently, our relationship feels more alive and expansive over time.

True intimacy is born out of love, not fear. When you're coming from fear, you keep certain parts of yourself hidden. When you're coming from love, you *want* to be vulnerable, as you know that a willingness to be vulnerable is essential for real intimacy.

To make a shift from fear to love in any circumstance, the first step is to develop the self-awareness necessary to notice when you're coming from fear. If you're feeling anxious, worried, or bored, you can be sure you're operating from a state of fear. Recognizing that you're coming from fear can provide the opening you need to ask yourself this transformational question: *What would it look like if I were coming from love right now?* This self-inquiry will help you see ways to approach the situation from a more effective, more loving place.

Team Up to Dissolve Your Fears

You and a close friend or partner can practice making the shift from fear to love anytime you have a few minutes together. Take a moment to identify anything you recognize you've been approaching from a place of fear. If you have trouble thinking of something, consider what you've recently been stressed, worried, anxious, or angry about.

Share with each other the fears you have identified. Then talk about what it might look like to approach each situation from a place of love instead. Be receptive as you both come up with possibilities. Your partner in this exercise may be very helpful here, as he or she may have a good sense of both you and your fear, without being caught up in the fear itself.

Just sharing your fears can be healing, as you're then no longer alone with them.

As you explore the various approaches, you'll likely experience a welcome wave of relief. You might also discover that a shift in this area of your life is already beginning to occur.

PRACTICE 4:
KNOW THAT WE'RE ALL CONNECTED

In every moment, we have the choice to see ourselves as separate from other people or to recognize that we are all connected.

Research in the field of quantum physics has revealed that, at the most fundamental level, we're all interconnected. Everything that exists is composed of the same energy, and every choice we make will affect ourselves and others in ways we can't even begin to predict.

Despite our interconnectedness, much of the time we act like we're entirely separate from one another. We tend to automatically view other people as our competitors rather than our companions. We evaluate, judge, and criticize them, instead of being open to who they are. At the same time, we hide who *we* really are rather than openly and honestly sharing ourselves, even with the people closest to us.

The more we recognize the truth that we're all connected, the more rewarding life becomes. Because we know that our actions can and do affect other people, we take more responsibility for our behavior. We become more compassionate, caring, and forgiving. We approach others with receptivity, and we share ourselves authentically. We feel increasingly connected to those around us and more and more passionate about our own lives.

Feel Your Connectedness to Everyone

To get a sense of your connectedness with all other people, start with your connection to just one person and expand from there. Begin by thinking of someone you know well, like a close friend. Then imagine all the people you're connected to through this person: their friends, their siblings, and the other people you've met as a result of knowing them. Contemplate this web of connections for a few moments.

> Take a walk with the intention of feeling your connection to everything around you.

Now recognize that everyone you're connected to through this friend is also connected to many other people. Visualize this network of connections expanding outward until it encompasses almost everyone on the planet. Feel what it's like to know that you are connected, in some small way, to nearly every other human being on earth.

Connect Through Your Eyes

Gazing into another person's eyes isn't only a romantic notion. It's also a powerful practice for experiencing a profoundly intimate sense of connection.

This can be done with your partner, a close friend, or even a stranger if you're both feeling safe and secure. Sit together in a quiet, warm, comfortable place. Hold hands if you like, and begin to look into each other's eyes. Let go of any effort and just allow yourselves to gaze comfortably.

As you gaze deeply into the other person's eyes, release any thoughts that come up. Even if new thoughts rush in to take their place, simply let go of each one and refocus your attention on your partner's eyes. Allow yourself to experience any feelings that arise—uneasiness, sadness, loss, joy, or even silliness—without trying to analyze them.

> Eye gazing is an inner journey that starts to dissolve the sense of separation between you and another.

Open yourself to being seen completely by this person and to seeing them in an entirely new way. If you allow yourself to fully relax, you'll notice a shift starting to take place. Issues that might have existed between you, or uncomfortable feelings you were having when you began, may start to fade away. You might find yourselves experiencing a much deeper sense of each other, and perhaps even a rich, warm, satisfying feeling that could be called pure love.

Connect Through an Embrace

Another way to feel your connection to another human being is through a hug in which you are both fully present. In this type of hug, which might last for several minutes or even longer, you allow yourself to really experience holding the other person and being held by them.

As you begin to relax into the embrace, allow any thoughts that come up, as well as any feelings of hesitation or resistance, to drift away. Bring your awareness to any parts of your body that are carrying tension, and consciously relax them as you exhale. Doing this will encourage your

> The more you relax into a hug, the more you will be able to sense your interconnectedness.

partner to relax further as well, which will in turn draw your own body into an even more relaxed state. Notice the rhythm of your partner's breathing and allow your own breath to synchronize with it. As you continue to let go into each other, you may have a sense that the two of you are almost merging together into one.

PRACTICE 5:
APPRECIATE EVERY MOMENT

In every moment, we have the choice to appreciate what life is bringing us or to be in complacency or even complaint about it.

It's not surprising that the more gratitude we feel for what we have, the happier, healthier, and more satisfied with our lives and relationships we become. Many of us, though, are in the habit of continually scanning for and focusing on "what's wrong." We're always on the lookout for what doesn't measure up to our ideas about how things should be.

Making a decision to notice "what's right" rather than "what's wrong" is something you do for *yourself*. That's because *in the moment you shift from complaint or complacency into gratitude, you instantly experience more harmony and love in your life.*

How do you raise your appreciation for what life is bringing you? By focusing more often on cherishing what you do have than on complaining about what you don't. By realizing that things could be worse. By recognizing that your time with your loved ones is precious and limited. By knowing that even in the face of challenging circumstances, you can find something to appreciate—if nothing more than the breath you're taking right now.

> When you express your appreciation by acknowledging others, you're giving them a gift of your gratitude.

Appreciate the Moments Together

The next time you go for a walk with your lover or a friend, do so with the idea of sharing with each other the everyday miracles you notice: a flower, laughter, the clouds in the sky, the way the sunlight radiates through the leaves.

As you walk, focus on enjoying the simple pleasure of being together. Appreciate that no matter where you've been or where you might be going, this person is here, experiencing life with you, right now.

Soul-to-soul connection isn't something you have to wait for;
you have the potential to create it in every encounter through the
choices you make every day. The more you incorporate the five
practices in this chapter into your life, the more joyful and rewarding
all your relationships will become. As you consciously and
consistently make these choices with another person, the connection
you feel will undoubtedly deepen. When you learn to truly accept
and appreciate yourself, other people, and the world in every moment,
you will be having a soulmate experience all the time.

Transformational Techniques
and Questions

Techniques for Creating Your Soulmate Experience

Techniques for Keeping Your Soulmate Experience Alive

Transformational Questions

Is there something we're both passionate about that we could contribute to the world—and, in the process, enhance our own relationship? 123

Will holding this resentment help me to create a relationship that is loving and connected? Am I willing to accept what I've been resenting in order to have a more fulfilling relationship experience? Is it possible that someone else could easily accept this about my partner? 131

What is there to appreciate about this being in my life? What opportunity is this situation presenting me? In what way could this situation actually contribute to my relationship? 138

What is there to appreciate about having this in our lives? What opportunity is this situation presenting us? How could this contribute to our relationship? 141

Is this the relationship I want to be in right now? If it is, what kind of person do I want to be in it? 185

What are the possible benefits of accepting what I'm currently resisting? 240

What would it look like if I were coming from love right now? 244

Discussion Questions

Introduction

Who have you felt connected to on a soul level, and how would you describe that connection? What are your beliefs about soulmates? What qualities do you believe will help attract a soulmate? What do you think might keep a soulmate experience alive?

Chapter 1: Changing Your Mind

What are some ways you've noticed your beliefs influencing your experience? What are your core beliefs, and how have they affected your life? How have your beliefs affected your relationships? What limiting beliefs have you let go of, and how were you able to release them? How did releasing these beliefs affect you? What other limiting beliefs are you ready to release?

Chapter 2: Loving Your Body

How have your feelings and beliefs about your body affected you? How have they affected your relationships? In what ways could you be more accepting, appreciative, caring, or loving toward your body?

Chapter 3: Reducing Your Baggage

How have you tried to address your own insufficiency conversation or feelings of low self-worth, and what has been most effective? In what ways have you avoided self-intimacy? What addictions or unhealthy habits are you ready to let go of? What are your special gifts, and how do you embrace and use them? What resentments are you ready to let go of?

Chapter 4: Raising Your Soulmate Potential

In what ways do you approach life in a spirit of discovery? What do you accept in life that others might resist, and what do you get from that acceptance? What gift or higher possibility have you discovered in a challenging circumstance or situation?

Chapter 5: Having a Guest in Your Life

What does it mean to you to treat a partner as a guest in your life? How do you recognize yourself in the descriptions of the conventional model and the soulmate model for relationship? How would you feel about being in a relationship that was based on the soulmate model? How do you practice gratitude in your life?

Chapter 6: Creating a Context

What requirements do you have for a relationship? What context, conscious or unconscious, have you held for your relationships? What context might you want to have for your relationships?

Chapter 7: Making Space

When you were growing up, how safe did you feel it was to be yourself? What do you think it would take to create a safe, loving space in your intimate relationship? How has resentment affected your relationships? What have you expanded to include in the past? What could you expand to include now?

Chapter 8: Turning Expectations into Invitations

In what ways have you been more open at the beginning of a relationship? In what ways have you opened up as a relationship developed? What expectations have you had of your partners, and what expectations have they had of you? In what ways have you seen expectations shut down a relationship? Can you identify an authentic desire beneath one of your expectations and find a way to express it as an invitation?

Chapter 9: Transforming the Energy of Jealousy

How has jealousy affected your relationships? What approaches have you taken toward jealousy, either yours or your partner's? In what ways could jealousy contribute to your relationship?

Chapter 10: Playing Leapfrog

How have you and a partner acted as each other's personal coach, spiritual teacher, or cheerleader? How do responsibility, trust, willingness, and transparency make playing leapfrog possible? In what ways have you played leapfrog with the people in your life? How might playing leapfrog with your partner enhance your relationship experience?

Chapter 11: Exploring the Edges

How have you contributed to making your relationships feel more alive? What are some ideas for date experiences that excite you? That make you nervous? In what ways have you issued a "default no" to someone else's passion? How might your experience have been different if you'd said yes? What does "relationship as a constant yes" mean to you?

Chapter 12: Connecting on a Soul Level

How do you practice accepting what is? How do you practice being right here, right now? How do you practice coming from a place of love? How do you practice knowing that we're all connected? How do you practice appreciation?

In Gratitude

We will be eternally grateful to the many beautiful souls who have encouraged, inspired, educated, and supported us during this heart-opening process.

Lana Apple, for your willingness to listen—and contribute!—to endless conversations about relationships. Thank you, LJ, for keeping us entertained, on our toes, and stocked up on vitamins.

Sarah Dunn, for your open mind and heart and for being so "comfortable in the world." And Ben Dunn, for teaching Joe many years ago how easy it is to let expectations get in the way of love.

Geoff Apple, for being Mali's loving wusband (not to mention bestowing her with such a cool last name). Geoff, in so many ways, this book is yours too. Marie Dunn, Joe's former partner, for exploring Michael Naumer's teachings with him. Marie, thank you for your love. And you both, for being open to doing relationships differently and being such loving parents to the children we share.

Chris Beyers, for demonstrating true unconditional love; thanks Mom! And Dick Dunn, for being Joe's biggest fan. Yes, Dad, writing a book is hard work.

Ken Keyes Jr., Richard Bach, Neale Donald Walsch, Eckhart Tolle, Caroline Myss, and Byron Katie, for sharing your enlightened consciousness with the world and helping us all to connect on a soul level. Ken, though we didn't have the opportunity to work together as planned, we feel you with us in spirit.

Michael Naumer, for knowing that there's always a higher possibility. Catherine Sevenau, for keeping Michael's light shining. And Christina Naumer (Alorah Inanna), for your transformative advice to "expand to include and have it contribute."

Anna Embree, for being our phenomenally intelligent, brilliantly irreverent, and eminently sensible editor. We just love you!

Kristi McCullough, for planting the seed of this book so long ago.

Eric Harr, for believing in our mission so completely when no one else even knew our names.

Diane Hart, for your guidance and encouragement during this "labor of mutual love."

Melody Anderson, Michael DeMarchi, Jeanne Hennessy, Galen Juhl, and Guy Tillotson, for ensuring this book didn't end up "soulless." Your love and wisdom are reflected on every page.

Laura Alavosus, Diane Knorr, Amy Zimmer, Paul Beyers, Rachel Farber, Joanne Sprott, and Deborah Newton, for giving of yourselves so generously. You will never know what enormous contributions you've made.

Deanna Dudney, our first-line reviewer, for being unwaveringly positive from the very first word and reminding us about the importance of intuition.

Arnold and Emily Stoper, Susan Kay and Kevin Fox, Ken and Linda Brown, and Don and Madeline Swartz, for your examples of what it means to be in love.

Dr. Adonis, for your professional, albeit anonymous, review and enthusiastic thumbs-up.

Abby Minot, for your boundless enthusiasm and on-call brilliance.

Karlyn Pipes-Neilsen, for helping to make the impossible possible.

Dawn Marrero, for always being open to seeing a higher possibility.

Hermine Terhorst, for your "constant yes."

Megan Monique Harner, for believing in us no matter what.

Ed Tucker, for always expressing the perfect thing, perfectly.

Rachel Balunsat, for demonstrating the power of compassion.

Edyta Saltsman, for being so willing to play.

Lauri Deits, for your insights into the little green monster.

Avasa Love, for lovingly encouraging us to own our gifts.

Anna Grace, for helping us express who we are.

Marybeth Giefer, for showing us what it means to hug.

John Sawicki, for teaching the importance of finding one's own way.

Matt Beyers, for your zero tolerance for typos.

For inspiration, encouragement, and generous support of various kinds: Lis Addison, Aji, Carlos "say what you mean" Anderson, Walter Bachtiger (love our hot tub debates!), Urszula "Superwoman" Balakier, Fran Bennett, Joel Beyers, Kerrin Beyers, Bert Bower, Andi Bradshaw, Laura Brewster, Sue Broadston, Matthew Brooks, Meghan Dunn Cawsey, Cathy Coe, Cassandra Coffee, Aaryn K. Coley-Gooden, Ray Coombs (yes, we can report progress!), René Couret,

Orann Crawford, Marie DeJournette, Wendy DeMos, Gayla D'Gaia, Nicole Doan, Jean Dunn, Maureen Moco Dunn, Rob Dunn, Tom Dunn, Matthew Dwyer, Bill Elbring, Ryland "Mr. Love" Englehart, Trenton "where's the love?" Farmer, Frank Ferrante, Buzz Foote, Tobin Giblin, Al Graham, Michael Guen, Kerrin Hartman, John Hatem, Robert Heath, Jim Hendrickson, Katharina and Jeromy Johnson, Michael Kane, Kimi Keating, Kyle Keller, Jeff Kelly, Katie Le Normand, Tracy Lubas, Susan Marjanovic, Stacey Miceli, Arpita Ohsiek, Avida Pappas, Kelly Phu, Kiran Rana, Maile Reilly, Cosmos Rennert, Margee Robinson, Karina Rousseau, Lynn Sanchez, Nancy Sawyer, Scott "ask me anything" Scheidt, Miles Smith, Wencil Storek, Joanie Rutman Tompkins, Nelson Young, and Lizzy Ziogas.

To the loving souls of Café Gratitude in San Rafael for appreciating life and being love in every moment.

To the many individuals who opened their hearts and shared their intimate stories, challenges, and successes with us. We're inspired by your courage, your willingness to approach relationships in new ways, and your desire to let others learn from your experience.

And finally, to the thousands of members and contributing artists of The Soulmate Experience community on Facebook, for demonstrating that the desire and willingness to connect on a soul level is alive and well.

We love you all!

Mali & Joe

Index

novelty, for keeping relationships alive, 96–98, 219–220
nudity, being comfortable with, 223, 224

online dating, 107–109
orbiting, 89–91

passion, sustaining, 87–88, 96–98, 151–152, 176, 188, 192–196, 215–236, 247–248
passions, exploring each other's, 232–235
pedestal, fall from, 144–146
"people are miraculous surprises" lens, 64–65
phobias, letting go of, 208
"playing at your edge," 218–223
presence, 22, 29, 96–98, 241–242
    practicing with a partner, 242–243, 248
promises, 110, 118–119

quantum physics, 245–246

reality, beliefs and, 4–16
regret
    causes of, 110, 241
    definition of, 59
    releasing, 59–66, 241–242
    see also resentment
rejection
    fear of, 49, 60, 127
    letting go of, 50–51, 60–66, 127–133
Relationships Research Institute, viii
replacement beliefs, 7–10, 19–25, 180–182, 190–191
reprogramming, 16–25, 180–182
resentment
    causes of, 9, 47, 66, 110, 129, 134, 148, 152–153, 171, 174–176, 178, 192, 216–217, 239, 241

definition of, 59
    preventing, 9–10, 67–68, 113, 133–142, 152, 218–219, 238–241, 242
    releasing, 59–66, 92–93, 128–133, 185–187, 192–194, 239–240
resignation, 86, 110
resistance, 15, 46, 74, 137–138, 151, 156, 200, 212, 238
    letting go of, 67–68, 72–75, 128, 138–141, 203, 233, 238–239
    see also acceptance
respect, 91, 192
responsibility, for self, 70, 87, 92, 97–98, 119, 177–178, 202, 246
rest, 42
romance, see passion
rules, 84, 118, 135, 171, 175

safe relationship space, 125–142, 162–163, 246
sarcasm, 157
security, 90, 107–108, 149, 170, 244
self-acceptance, 27, 29–40, 48–51, 63–64, 174, 179
self-appreciation, 27, 29, 31–40, 42
self-awareness, 71–72, 75, 95, 135, 152–153, 239–240, 244
    developing greater, 14–16, 21, 42–43, 45–66
self-criticism, 27–31, 33–34, 36, 38–39, 239
    effect on relationships, 28–29, 31
    quieting, 32–33, 34–38, 39–40, 239–240
self-discovery, 71–73, 127–128
self-esteem, 13, 32, 51, 53–54, 181, 185
self-image, 27–40, 43
self-intimacy, 48–51
self-responsibility, 70, 87, 92, 97–98, 119, 177–178, 202, 246

Join The Soulmate Experience on Facebook®

The Soulmate Experience is more than just a book. It's also a community of loving people from around the world who are sharing themselves and their experiences and connecting with others on deeper, more meaningful levels. Join the ongoing inspirational conversations at www.Facebook.com/TheSoulmateExperience. Who knows? You just might meet your soulmate here!

"I love this site. It has given me much more power to be the person I wanted to be a long time ago." ~DANA RATCLIFFE

"My friends here at The Soulmate Experience help me more than they know." ~DENISE COMBS VANSCIVER

"Provocative and powerful, this site has changed me in so many ways. I am more mindful, present, and soulful. I also met a lovely woman here and have never experienced such deep, soulful love in my five decades of life." ~MIKE PASLEY

"This site is a blessing to me—like therapy on some days and a source of encouragement *every* day." ~DIANE BETTON

"This is quite the community of loving souls gathered here. Thank you for creating a safe place for us to explore our soulful expressions." ~DAVIE HANNAFORD

"I am so happy I found this community! I have been truly blessed with new friendships that have touched my heart... one in particular..." ~SUZANNE CROSS NEWCOMB

"The people who share their wisdom, inspiration, truth, experiences, hope, and joy on this site assist me daily. God did not send me a guardian angel. He sent me a flock." ~GERRY CARDINALLI

Visit Us Online

Come to www.TheSoulmateExperience.com for news about events, workshops, and new books in *The Soulmate Experience* series.